Crystallization-Study
of
Revelation

Volume One

Witness Lee

The Holy Word for Morning Revival

Living Stream Ministry
Anaheim, California

First Edition, July 1999.

ISBN 0-7363-0712-5

Published by

Living Stream Ministry
2431 W. La Palma Ave., Anaheim, CA 92801 U.S.A.
P. O. Box 2121, Anaheim, CA 92814 U.S.A.

Printed in the United States of America

99 00 01 02 03 04 05 / 10 9 8 7 6 5 4 3 2 1

Contents

Preface

1. This book is intended as an aid to believers in developing a daily time of morning revival with the Lord in His word. At the same time, it provides a review of the 1999 Summer Training on the "Crystallization-study of Revelation." Through intimate contact with the Lord in His word, the believers can be constituted with life and truth and thereby equipped to prophesy in the meetings of the church unto the building up of the Body of Christ.

2. The content of this book is taken primarily from the *Crystallization-study Outlines,* the text and footnotes of the Recovery Version of the Bible, selections from the writings of Watchman Nee and Witness Lee, and *Hymns,* all of which are published by Living Stream Ministry.

3. The book is divided into weeks. One training message is covered per week. Each week first presents the message outline, followed by six daily portions, a hymn, and then some space for writing. The message outline has been divided into days, corresponding to the six daily portions. Each daily portion covers certain points and begins with a section entitled "Morning Nourishment." This section contains selected verses and a short reading that can provide rich spiritual nourishment through intimate fellowship with the Lord. The "Morning Nourishment" is followed by a section entitled "Today's Reading," a longer portion of ministry related to the day's main points. Each day's portion concludes with a short list of references for further reading and some space for the saints to make notes concerning their spiritual inspiration, enlightenment, and enjoyment to serve as a reminder of what they have received of the Lord that day.

4. The space provided at the end of each week is for composing a short prophecy. This prophecy can be composed by considering all our daily notes, the "harvest" of our inspirations during the week, and preparing a main point with some sub-points to be spoken in the church meetings for the organic building up of the Body of Christ.

5. The *Crystallization-study Outlines* were compiled by Living Stream Ministry from the writings of Watchman Nee and Witness Lee. The outlines, footnotes, and references in the Recovery Version of the Bible were written by Witness Lee. All of the other references cited in this publication are from the ministry of Watchman Nee and Witness Lee.

1999 Summer Training

CRYSTALLIZATION-STUDY
OF REVELATION

Banners:

Christ, the worthy and enthroned Lion-Lamb,
is the heavenly Administrator
in the divine government,
opening the scroll of God's economy
to unlock the secret of the universe.

We need to subjectively experience
the detailed aspects of the golden lampstand,
so that we can become
the reproduction of the lampstand,
the expression of the Triune God.

The overcomers,
produced through the intensification
of God's organic salvation
by Christ as the sevenfold intensified Spirit,
conquer the satanic chaos
and triumph in the divine economy.

We need to follow the Lamb wherever He may go
to preach the gospel of the kingdom
to the whole inhabited earth
for the propagation and development
of the seed, the gene, of the kingdom
to consummate this age.

An Introductory Word and the Unique and Ultimate Revelation of Jesus Christ

Scripture Reading: Rev. 1:1-3, 13; 4:5; 5:5-6; 21:2, 23

Day 1
I. An introductory word:

A. Revelation is a book of signs (1:1):

1. The word *signs* in 1:1 is the key to interpret the entire book of Revelation (12:1, 3; 15:1).

2. The God-given revelation in this book is made known by signs, that is, by symbols with a spiritual significance.

3. In the book of Revelation, which is composed of signs, there are two great signs—the sign of the golden lampstands and the sign of the New Jerusalem (1:12, 20; 2:1; 21:2, 10).

B. Revelation is a book of prophecy (1:3; 22:7, 10, 18a):

1. The revelation in this book is in the nature of prophecy, with most of the visions referring to things to come (1:19).

2. The prophecy in this book is not merely in words but also in visions revealed to the seer (1:2, 11a).

3. In the eyes of God, all the things prophesied in this book have already taken place (21:6a).

Day 2
C. Revelation is a book of administration (4:2, 5; 5:6):

1. The book of Revelation presents a clear view of God's universal administration (4:2-3).

2. The subject of Revelation is Christ as the center of God's administration according to God's eternal economy (5:6; 22:1).

D. Revelation is a book of consummation (21:1-2):

1. The consummation of the divine revelation (22:18-19).

Day 3

2. The consummation of the divine economy with the divine dispensing (22:17, 1-2).

3. The consummation of the two trees, the two sources, the two lines, and the two principles (20:10, 14-15; 21:8, 2, 10; 22:1-2, 14, 17b).

4. The consummation of the entire Bible with its governing principle—the Triune God wrought into the tripartite man (21:18, 21, 19a, 11).

E. Revelation is a book of intensification (1:4; 3:1; 4:5; 5:6):

1. The full ministry of Christ is in three stages—incarnation, inclusion, and intensification (John 1:14; 1 Cor. 15:45; Rev. 1:4).

2. In Revelation the Spirit is the seven Spirits, the sevenfold intensified Spirit (3:1; 4:5; 5:6).

3. In 1:4-5 the Spirit becomes the second, the center, of the Divine Trinity, revealing the importance of the intensified function of the sevenfold Spirit of God.

Day 4

II. **The book of Revelation is the unique and ultimate revelation of Jesus Christ (1:1a):**

A. The unique and ultimate revelation of Jesus Christ is a revelation of the all-inclusiveness of Christ:

1. Jesus as Jehovah the Savior and Christ as the One anointed by God to carry out His economy (1:1a).

2. The faithful Witness (1:5; 3:14).

3. The Firstborn of the dead (1:5).

4. The Son of God and the Son of Man (2:18; 1:13).

5. The First and the Last, the Beginning and the End, the Alpha and the Omega (1:17; 2:8; 22:13).

6. The living One (1:18).

7. The Holy One and the true One (3:7).

8. The faithful One (19:11).

9. The Amen (3:14).

10. The beginning of the creation of God (3:14).

11. The Root and the Offspring of David (5:5; 22:16).

12. The Lion and the Lamb (5:5-6; 21:23; 22:1).

13. Another Angel (7:2; 8:3; 10:1; 18:1).

14. King of kings and Lord of lords (19:16; 17:14).

15. The Word of God (19:13).

16. The morning star (22:16; 2:28).

17. The lamp (21:23).

18. The Husband (21:2; 19:9a).

Day 5

B. The unique and ultimate revelation of Jesus Christ is a revelation of Christ in the stage of intensification (5:6):

1. Christ as the life-giving Spirit has been intensified to be the seven Spirits, the sevenfold intensified Spirit (2:1, 7a; 3:1; 4:5; 5:6).

2. Christ's ministry in the stage of intensification is to intensify His organic salvation, to produce the overcomers, and to consummate the New Jerusalem as the goal of God's economy.

Day 6

C. The unique and ultimate revelation of Jesus Christ is a revelation of Christ in the divine administration (5:6; 22:1):

1. In the divine administration Christ is the Ruler of the kings of the earth, ruling the whole earth that the gospel may be spread and that the churches may be produced (1:5).

2. In the divine administration Christ is the High Priest, judging and purifying the churches and holding the messengers of the churches (1:13, 16a, 20; 2:1).

3. In the divine administration Christ is the worthy Lion-Lamb, the overcoming Redeemer, opening the scroll of God's economy (5:3-7).

D. The unique and ultimate revelation of Jesus
Christ is a revelation of Christ in His ascension, in His coming back, in His judgment, in
His possessing the earth, in His reigning in
the kingdom, and in His centrality and univer-
sality in eternity (5:6; 3:3b; 1:7; 15:1; 18:1;
20:4, 6; 21:23).

Morning Nourishment

Rev. **The revelation of Jesus Christ which God gave**
1:1 **to Him to show to His slaves the things that must**
     quickly take place; and He made *it* known by
     signs, sending *it* by His angel to His slave John.
12 **...And when I turned, I saw seven golden lamp-**
     stands.
21:2 **And I saw the holy city, New Jerusalem, coming**
     down out of heaven from God....
5-6 **...Write, for these words are faithful and true.**
     And He said to me, They have come to pass....

[In Revelation 1:1] we see that the divine revelation is given to Jesus Christ and that He makes it known by signs. All the pictures in Revelation are signs. The revelation in the book of Revelation is composed mainly of signs, that is, symbols with spiritual significance, such as the seven lampstands signifying the churches and the seven stars signifying the messengers of the churches (1:20). Even the New Jerusalem is a sign, signifying the ultimate consummation of God's economy. This book, then, is a book of signs, symbols through which the revelation is made known to us. John's Gospel is a book of signs signifying how Christ came to be our life to produce the church, His bride. John's Revelation is also a book of signs showing how Christ is now caring for the church and how He is coming to judge and possess the earth and to bring the church, His bride, into God's full economy. (*Life-study of the New Testament, Conclusion Messages,* p. 2687)

Today's Reading

Revelation is a book of prophecy (1:3; 22:7), for the revelation it contains is in the nature of prophecy. Most of the visions refer to things to come. Even the seven epistles to the seven churches in chapters two and three, in the sense of signs, are prophecies regarding the church on earth until the Lord's coming back. Although this book is a book of prophecy, it is not prophecy merely in words, but in visions revealed to the seer. In the eyes of God, all the things prophesied in this book have already transpired and all have been shown to the seer in vision after vision.

In the book of Revelation, most of the verbs and predicates are not in the future tense, but in the past tense, indicating that the events recorded in this book have already transpired. Strictly speaking, Revelation is not merely a prophecy; it is a revelation of things which have already taken place. While they may not seem in our eyes to have transpired, in God's eyes they have transpired. In God's eyes, everything recorded in this book occurred nearly two thousand years ago. We all must believe this.

In Revelation, two main things have transpired. The first is that the testimony of Jesus has been accomplished for eternity....The New Jerusalem, the ultimate consummation of God's work through the centuries, has been completely built up, and we are in it! According to the last two chapters of Revelation, the building of the New Jerusalem has been accomplished. This first item is on the positive side.

On the negative side, a second main thing has transpired— Satan, the enemy of God, has been dealt with. In the eyes of God and even in the eyes of our brother John, Satan has been cast into the lake of fire (20:10). Satan, the serpent, is in the lake of fire, and we are in the New Jerusalem. Have you seen this? If we have seen that Satan is in the lake of fire, we shall not beg God to deal with him. Rather, we shall praise Him that the enemy has been dealt with.

The book of Revelation has been closed because it exposes Satan, disclosing his destiny and destination. But now, at the end of time, we believe that the Lord will open up this book and open up our hearts, spirits, and eyes that we may clearly see that God's enemy is now in the lake of fire. Hallelujah, Satan, the old serpent, is in the lake of fire and we are in the New Jerusalem! (*Life-study of Revelation*, pp. 1-3)

Further Reading: Life-study of the New Testament, Conclusion Messages, msg. 257; Life-study of Revelation, msg. 1; Elders' Training, Book 2: The Vision of the Lord's Recovery, ch. 5; The Central Line of the Divine Revelation, msg. 28

Enlightenment and inspiration: _____

_____

Morning Nourishment

Rev. ...Send forth Your sickle and reap, for the hour
14:15 to reap has come because the harvest of the earth
is ripe.
21:1-2 And I saw a new heaven and a new earth; for the
first heaven and the first earth passed away, and
the sea is no more. And I saw the holy city, New
Jerusalem, coming down out of heaven from God,
prepared as a bride adorned for her husband.

The book of Revelation also presents a wonderful and
marvelous consummation of the church. In this book we see
God's economy, Christ's redemption, and the church's testimony. Without Revelation, we could read the Epistles again
and again without realizing that the church is Christ's testimony. In which of the Epistles do we see the churches shining
as lampstands in the dark night? Only in the book of Revelation do we see this. In Revelation, the churches firstly are the
shining lampstands. Eventually, in eternity, the church will be
the New Jerusalem, a golden mountain. This is the wonderful
consummation of the church. (*Life-study of Revelation*, pp. 5-6)

Today's Reading

If we did not have the book of Revelation, we would not know
what Satan's destiny is, and no one would be able to understand why God has been and still is tolerating the subtle, evil,
dirty Satan. However, if we get into this book and see the
conclusion of Satan's record, we shall be happy and laugh at
the serpent. Therefore, in Revelation we have the conclusion
of four major things—God's economy, Christ's redemption, the
church's testimony, and Satan's destiny.

Revelation is also the conclusion of the New Testament,
which is composed of the Gospels, the Acts, the Epistles, and
Revelation. In the Gospels we see the sowing of the seed of life,
for in the Gospels Jesus came to sow Himself into humanity
as the seed of life, sowing Himself into a small number of

people, such as Peter and John. In the Acts is the propagation of life. In the Epistles we see the growth of life. The central concept of all the Epistles written by Paul, Peter, John, and the others is the growth of life. We all need to grow in life. In Revelation we see, once again, the harvest of life. In chapter fourteen of Revelation we have a ripened field and a harvest [Rev. 14:15]....In Revelation 14, the whole field is harvested. By this we see that Revelation is the conclusion of the New Testament.

As the last book of the Bible, Revelation is the conclusion, completion, and consummation of the entire divine revelation, the whole Bible. The Bible needs such a conclusion. The seeds of most of the truths of the divine revelation were sown in Genesis, the first book of the Bible. The growth of all these seeds is progressively developed in the following books, especially in the books of the New Testament, and the harvest is reaped in the book of Revelation. For example, in Genesis is the seed of the serpent, and in the book of Revelation there is the harvest of the serpent. Hence, most of the things covered in this book are not absolutely new, but refer back to the foregoing books of the Bible. In Genesis is the seed of the divine revelation, in the following books is the progressive development of the divine revelation, and in Revelation is the harvest of the divine revelation. Therefore, we all must get into this book and know it. If we do not know this book, we cannot be clear about God's revelation. In our travels, we often are not clear about the way, the road, until we have reached our destination. After we have reached our destination and look back upon the way we have taken, we become very clear. In Revelation we arrive at the destination of the whole Bible. Having arrived at this destination, we can understand this divine Book. (*Life-study of Revelation,* pp. 6-8)

Further Reading: Life-study of Revelation, msg. 1; *Concerning the Lord's Recovery,* ch. 6

Enlightenment and inspiration: _____
_____
_____
_____

Morning Nourishment

Rev. **And he showed me a river of water of life, bright as**
22:1-2 **crystal, proceeding out of the throne of God and of**
      the Lamb in the middle of its street. And on this side
      and on that side of the river was the tree of life....
  14 **Blessed are those who wash their robes that they**
      may have right to the tree of life and may enter by
      the gates into the city.

The destination of God's way of life is a city of water of life, the New Jerusalem, God's eternal dwelling (Rev. 21:2, 11, 23; 22:1-2, 14), as the best and most glorious goal for all the men who walk in the way of life according to God's desire and for God's pleasure, that they may participate with God in all the blessings of God as the eternal life for eternity.

The destination of the way of death and of good and evil is a lake of fire and brimstone, the Gehenna of fire (Matt. 5:22), Satan's eternal prison, as the worst and most miserable end for all the men who take the way of death according to Satan's evil device, that they may share with Satan the eternal judgment and eternal perdition (John 16:11; Matt. 25:41; Rev. 21:8, 27; 22:15).

The New Jerusalem, as the best and most glorious end of God's way of life, is a dynamic incentive for us to seek God until we gain Him to the fullest extent according to His love and grace; and the lake of fire, as the worst and most miserable end of Satan's way of death and of good and evil, should be a solemn warning to the men who follow Satan in his way against God's economy, to turn from his way of death to God's way of life that they may escape Satan's eternal judgment and eternal perdition, according to God's righteousness and justice. (*Life-study of Job*, pp. 203-204)

Today's Reading

The New Testament revelation shows us the Triune God and how He has gone through the processes to become the all-inclusive, life-giving Spirit to work Himself into us to become our life, our life supply, and our everything. Such a dispensing of the Triune

God into His chosen and redeemed people will consummate in the New Jerusalem, which is a mutual dwelling place for Him and for His redeemed ones. This is the basic line of the New Testament revelation according to God's entire economy. To interpret the house in John and the city in Revelation as physical things would mean that they have nothing to do with the basic line of the New Testament revelation. This interpretation eventually robs the riches of the divine revelation and annuls all the proper principles of biblical interpretation, so we lose everything. The heart and the pulse of the New Testament ministry is lost, is gone. The house in John and the city in Revelation must be brought back to their rightful position in God's New Testament economy. Both are the very illustration of the Triune God working Himself into our being to be the house and to be the city. In the house and in the city the Divine Trinity is fully portrayed.

John 14 through 17 is a great section of the New Testament telling us the details concerning the Triune God dispensing Himself in His Divine Trinity into our entire being. The ultimate consummation of the Triune God dispensing Himself into our being is this holy city, the New Jerusalem. This is not merely an interpretation of the Bible. What we have shared is very basic and very crucial. The Triune God is being dispensed into us to produce the house and to produce the city. The house is the result of the Triune God's dispensing and the city is the consummation of this result.

The entire Bible was written according to the principle of the Triune God wrought into His redeemed people as their enjoyment, their drink, and their fountain of life and light. The application of this principle in interpreting any portion of the New Testament is endless....Our basis of interpretation is the principle of the vision of the Triune God being wrought into our being. This really makes a difference. *(Elders' Training, Book 2: The Vision of the Lord's Recovery,* pp. 149-150, 168, 170)

Further Reading: Life-study of Job, msg. 37; *Elders' Training, Book 2: The Vision of the Lord's Recovery,* chs. 10-13

Enlightenment and inspiration: _____

_____

Morning Nourishment

Rev. **And the living One; and I became dead, and**
1:18 **behold, I am living forever and ever; and I have**
      the keys of death and of Hades.
22:13 **I am the Alpha and the Omega, the First and the**
       Last, the Beginning and the End.

[The book of Revelation] tells us that Christ is the ancient One, for His hair is exceedingly white. White hair, humanly speaking, always signifies oldness, but here it signifies that Christ is the ancient One. No one is as ancient as He. But this does not mean that He is old. He is ancient, yet He is so living. "I am...the living One" (Rev. 1:17-18).

The older we are, the more living we must be. We, the older ones, must be more living. Christ is the most ancient One, yet He is the most living One. He is living for evermore. He is ancient and He is living.

I have known some local churches who were very living when they first began to meet, but after two or three years they became old. This is wrong. The older a church is, the more living it must be. The church must be as Christ, the Head. He is the oldest, the most ancient, yet He is the most living. I hope that as the church in Los Angeles grows older, it will also become more and more living. (*The Seven Spirits for the Local Churches,* p. 59)

Today's Reading

The Son is the First and the Last (1:17; 2:8; 22:13), the Beginning and the End (22:13), and the Alpha and the Omega (22:13). When I was young, I was bothered by these terms, thinking that they were repetitious and that the Beginning, the First, and the Alpha were the same and that the End, the Last, and the Omega were the same. But this is not a matter of repetition, but of different aspects. Being the first does not necessarily mean that you are the end. Being the first simply means that you are the first and that prior to you there was nothing. However, to be the beginning does not only mean that you are the first, but also that you have begun something. What then is the difference between the Alpha and the beginning? A certain thing may be the beginning, but it may have neither the content nor the continuation. To be the Alpha and the Omega means that you are the complete content and continuation. For Christ to be the Alpha and the Omega, the first and last letters of the Greek alphabet, indicates that He is also every other letter in the alphabet. The first and the last simply indicate the first and the last without indicating either the beginning or the ending. In order to be the beginning and the ending, you must take a certain action. Christ is not only the first but also the beginning, the beginning of God's economy and God's operation. God's operation began and will end with Christ. This Christ is also the content and continuation of God's operation, because He is not only the beginning and the ending but also the Alpha and the Omega. In other words, the Son, Jesus Christ, is everything. He is the first and the last, the beginning and the ending of God's operation, and the content and continuation of whatever God is doing. Because the Greek letters from Alpha to Omega comprise all the letters of the Greek alphabet, we may say that Christ is every letter for us to compose words, sentences, paragraphs, chapters, and books. Hallelujah, He is everything! (*Life-study of Revelation,* pp. 45-46)

Further Reading: The Seven Spirits for the Local Churches, ch. 6; *Life-study of Revelation,* msgs. 2, 4; *Christ Revealed in the New Testament,* ch. 4; *The Divine Dispensing of the Divine Trinity,* ch. 10; *The Stream,* vol. 14, no. 3, pp. 1522-1528

Enlightenment and inspiration: _____

_____

_____

_____

Morning Nourishment

Rev. **And to the messenger of the church in Sardis write:**
3:1 **These things says He who has the seven Spirits of God....**
4:5 **...And *there were* seven lamps of fire burning before the throne, which are the seven Spirits of God.**
5:6 **And I saw in the midst of the throne...a Lamb standing as having *just* been slain, having seven horns and seven eyes, which are the seven Spirits of God sent forth into all the earth.**

My use of the word *inclusion* is based on our use of the word *inclusive.* For the last Adam to become the life-giving Spirit was for Christ to become the all-inclusive Spirit. His becoming all-inclusive was a matter not just of incarnation but of inclusion. As we have pointed out, inclusion involves many complications. In the stage of inclusion, many things are included in the pneumatic Christ, in the Christ who is the life-giving Spirit. Now we need to see that the all-inclusive, life-giving Spirit has been intensified sevenfold.

I would urge you to consider this matter of intensification and to pray desperately, saying, "Lord, I must advance. I need Your grace to bring me onward. I do not want to remain in the work of incarnation nor even in the work of inclusion. I want to advance from inclusion to intensification. Lord, You have been intensified sevenfold, and I pray that I also will be intensified sevenfold to overcome the degradation of the church that the Body may be built up to consummate the New Jerusalem." (*Incarnation, Inclusion, and Intensification,* p. 22)

Today's Reading

Recently, I have often repented and prayed, "Lord, I am in fear and trembling about one thing, that is, that from the past until the present, I am still not an overcomer. Lord, I pray that You would give me a few more years and measure to me another length of time in which I can exercise to become one of Your overcomers." Today we dare not say who are overcomers and who are not. We can only wait for His return when we will stand before His judgment seat, and He will judge whether we have overcome or have been defeated (2 Cor. 5:10; Rom. 14:10). The overcoming ones will enter into the kingdom with Him to reign as kings; the defeated ones will go to the outer darkness to be chastened for one thousand years (Matt. 25:21, 23, 30). Sooner or later we all have to mature. If we do not mature in this age, we will be put into the darkness in the coming age to be chastised so that we may become mature. After the one thousand years, all the believers will have become mature to be the overcomers (Rev. 21:7), who will be qualified to participate in the New Jerusalem. The New Jerusalem in the kingdom age is of a small scale, being constituted only with the overcomers in this age. After the kingdom is over, after the majority of the believers as the defeated ones have suffered chastisement in the darkness, they will have become mature and will be qualified to participate in the New Jerusalem in its consummation. This is the pure revelation of the holy Word.

In His seven epistles to the degraded churches, Christ is calling the defeated believers to be His overcomers by Himself as the sevenfold intensified Spirit for their experience of His organic salvation in His sevenfold intensification. I can testify that this is a reality. It has not been until recent years, especially the last three years, that I know in a deep way what God's organic salvation is. Furthermore, this organic salvation is strengthening me from within. In such a sevenfold-intensified organic salvation, we can become overcomers by Christ as the sevenfold intensified Spirit. *(How to Be a Co-worker and an Elder and How to Fulfill Their Obligations,* pp. 48-49)

Further Reading: Incarnation, Inclusion, and Intensification, chs. 1-2; *How to Be a Co-worker and an Elder and How to Fulfill Their Obligations,* ch. 3

Enlightenment and inspiration: _____

_____

_____

Morning Nourishment

Rev. ...If therefore you will not watch, I will come as
3:3   a thief, and you shall by no means know at what
      hour I will come upon you.
5:5   And one of the elders said to me, Do not weep;
      behold, the Lion of the tribe of Judah, the Root
      of David, has overcome so that He may open the
      scroll and its seven seals.

No book reveals Christ's coming back as clearly as the
book of Revelation does. This book reveals that Christ's
coming back has two aspects—a secret aspect and a public
aspect. This is possible because Christ is wonderful. Firstly,
Christ will come back secretly as a thief (3:3b; 16:15). No thief
tells you in advance the time of his arrival. In His secret
coming as a thief, Christ will come to steal the precious
things. No thief steals things that are without value. Thieves
only come to steal what is valuable. Christ tells us to be
watchful, saying, "If therefore you will not watch, I will come
as a thief, and you shall by no means know at what hour I
will come upon you" (3:3b). The time of His secret coming is
unknown. We all must ask ourselves, "Am I precious? Am I
worthy of being stolen by Christ in His secret coming?"
(*Life-study of Revelation,* pp. 20-21)

Today's Reading

Our Savior is the Lamb as well as the Lion. We have a
Lion-Lamb Savior. This One is worthy to open the scroll.
Apart from Him, no one in the universe is worthy to open the
secret, the mystery, of God's economy. But the Lion-Lamb is
worthy because He has accomplished redemption and has
won the victory over Satan. Whenever we Christians have
said that Christ was worthy, our thought was that He was
worthy of our praises and thanks and worship. When we said,
"Lord Jesus, You are worthy," not many of us realized that He
was worthy to open the seals of the secret of God's economy.

We only had the concept that Christ was worthy to receive worship, praise, and thanks from us, His little creatures. But this is an inadequate concept of the Lord's worthiness. Yet most hymns on the worthiness of Christ express this inadequate concept of His worthiness. Not many hymns praise Christ for being worthy to open the secret of God's economy. This aspect of the Lord's worthiness is universal and immeasurable. Of course, Christ is worthy of our praises. He is even worthy of our lives. Nevertheless, we must realize that, according to Revelation 5, Christ's worthiness is a matter of His being worthy to open the secret of God's economy. The universe is a mystery which the scientists cannot unravel. They simply do not know the meaning or the purpose of the universe, because it is a secret kept from them. But Christ is worthy to open this secret for He is worthy to open the seals of God's economy.

Revelation 5:5 says that the Lion is worthy to open the scroll and its seven seals. A scroll is a roll of parchment paper or other material. Because a scroll is rolled up, it is difficult to determine just how long it is. The scroll in Revelation 5 is eternally long. Only Christ is worthy to open this eternally-long scroll. Do not think that you have seen everything contained in this scroll. No, we shall need eternity to see all that is included in it. When we are in the New Jerusalem, we shall still be reading the contents of the scroll. For eternity we shall say, "Now I see something more." God will give us an eternal surprise. The surprise of the opening of the scroll will last for eternity. When you are in eternity, you may say, "The Lord's surprise is eternal. Although we are now in eternity, we still cannot see the end." Christ is worthy to open this scroll of God's mystery. (*Life-study of Revelation,* pp. 17-18)

Further Reading: Life-study of Revelation, msg. 2; *Life-study of the New Testament, Conclusion Messages,* msg. 31*

Enlightenment and inspiration: _____

_____

_____

_____

_____

Hymns, #132

1   Lo! in heaven Jesus sitting,
      Christ the Lord is there enthroned;
    As the man by God exalted,
      With God's glory He is crowned.

2   He hath put on human nature,
      Died according to God's plan,
    Resurrected with a body,
      And ascended as a man.

3   God in Him on earth was humbled,
      God with man was domiciled;
    Man in Him in heav'n exalted,
      Man with God is reconciled.

4   He as God with man is mingled,
      God in man is testified;
    He as man with God is blended,
      Man in God is glorified.

5   From the Glorified in heaven
      The inclusive Spirit came;
    All of Jesus' work and Person
      Doth this Spirit here proclaim.

6   With the Glorified in heaven
      Is the church identified;
    By the Spirit of this Jesus
      Are His members edified.

7   Lo! a man is now in heaven
      As the Lord of all enthroned;
    This is Jesus Christ our Savior,
      With God's glory ever crowned!

Composition for prophecy with main point and sub-points: _____

_____
_____
_____
_____
_____
_____
_____
_____
_____
_____
_____
_____
_____
_____
_____
_____
_____
_____
_____
_____
_____
_____
_____
_____
_____
_____
_____
_____
_____
_____
_____
_____
_____
_____

The Word of God and the Testimony of Jesus

Scripture Reading: Rev. 1:1-2, 9; 6:9; 12:17; 19:10, 13; 20:4

Day 1 I. **The book of Revelation presents to us the revealed Christ and the testifying church (1:1-2, 9; 6:9; 12:17; 20:4; 19:13):**

A. Christ as the Word of God is the testimony of God, the Witness of God, the definition, explanation, and expression of the mysterious and invisible God, the One who reveals God to us (John 1:1, 14, 18; Rev. 1:5; cf. Exo. 25:21-22).

B. The church as the Body of Christ, consummating in the New Jerusalem, is the testimony, the expression, of Christ; as such, the church is the reproduction of the testimony, the expression, of God in Christ (Eph. 1:22-23; Rev. 21:2-3; cf. Exo. 38:21).

C. Our enjoyment of the revealed Christ as the testimony of God constitutes us into His testimony, which is the present revelation of Jesus Christ (1 Tim. 3:15-16).

Day 2 II. **Christ as the Word of God is in three forms— the person of Christ Himself, the spoken word, and the written word (John 1:1; 5:39-40; 6:63):**

A. Christ as the testimony of God and the living word of God infuses His substance into His loving seekers, working Himself into them to make them His enlarged and expanded testimony:

1. Through the Word we can enjoy God's countenance and the shining of His face so that we can glow with Him for His glory (Exo. 34:28-29; 2 Cor. 3:16, 18; Psa. 27:4, 8; Psa. 119:58, 135).

2. By pray-reading the Word, we breathe God's element into us, being infused with what God is to cause us to live Christ and

become the living expression of God (2 Tim. 3:16-17; Eph. 6:17-18).

Day 3

3. We need to let the word of Christ inhabit us richly, singing His word, so that His word may enlighten us, nourish us, quench our thirst, strengthen us, wash us, build us up, perfect us, edify us, and fill us with joy (Col. 3:16; Psa. 119:54; cf. 1 Kings 6:7; 1 Chron. 6:31-32).

4. Our life as believers hinges totally upon the Lord's speaking—His instant, present, living word to sanctify us, preparing us to be His glorious bride (Eph. 5:25-27; cf. S. S. 6:13; 8:13-14).

Day 4

B. Christ as the Word of God is the Warrior of God with His bridal army as His testimony to execute God's judgment upon the man of lawlessness and the armies who follow him by the sharp sword, the almighty word that proceeds out of His mouth (Rev. 19:13, 15):

1. The sword which proceeds out of the mouth of Christ, who is the Word of God, is the word which will judge the rebellious (vv. 15, 21; John 12:48).

2. His fighting is the speaking of God's word; as the Lord fights, He speaks for God and expresses God (Rev. 2:16).

3. The Lord Jesus as the Word of God will slay the man of lawlessness by the breath of His mouth and bring him to nothing by the manifestation of His coming (2 Thes. 2:3-8; 1 John 3:4).

Day 5

4. In this age we need to receive the word as the Spirit, which then becomes a sword to slay the adversary within us, applying Ephesians 6:17-18 in an experiential way:

a. Without the word as the Spirit to be the killing sword, there is no way for us to be kept in the church life and in the ministry.

b. The word that we receive in a living way as the Spirit is a spiritual antibiotic that kills the "germs" within us so that the evil forces in the air have no way to take advantage of us.

5. Christ as the living word infuses us with God's substance, and Christ as the slaying word kills the adversary within us to make us His overcoming testimony for the accomplishment of His eternal economy, the fulfillment of His original intention (Gen. 1:26).

Day 6 **III. The testimony of Jesus is the spirit—the reality, substance, disposition, and characteristic—of the prophecy of the book of Revelation (Rev. 19:10):**

A. The testimony of Jesus is the seven golden lampstands as the shining churches—divine in nature, shining in darkness, and identical with one another (1:11-20).

B. The testimony of Jesus is the great multitude serving God in the temple, the whole Body of God's redeemed, who have been raptured to the heavens to enjoy God's care and the Lamb's shepherding (7:9-17).

C. The testimony of Jesus is the bright woman, representing the whole Body of God's redeemed, with her man-child, representing the overcomers as the stronger part of God's people (12:1-17).

D. The testimony of Jesus is the firstfruits, signifying the overcomers raptured before the great tribulation, and the harvest, signifying the majority of the believers who will be raptured at the end of the great tribulation (14:1-5, 14-16).

E. The testimony of Jesus is the victorious ones standing on the glassy sea, signifying the late overcomers who will pass through the great tribulation and overcome Antichrist and the worshipping of Antichrist (15:2-4).

F. The testimony of Jesus is the bride ready for marriage, consisting of the overcoming saints during the millennium (19:7-9).

G. The testimony of Jesus is the bridal army to fight along with Christ, the embodiment of God, and defeat the Antichrist, the embodiment of Satan, with his armies (vv. 14-19; 17:14).

H. Ultimately, the testimony of Jesus is the New Jerusalem, the great universal, divine-human incorporation of the processed and consummated Triune God with His regenerated, transformed, and glorified tripartite people (Rev. 21:2-3, 22; cf. Exo. 38:21) and the unique lampstand as the consummation of all the lampstands for the consummate expression of God (Rev. 21:18, 23; 22:5).

Morning Nourishment

Rev. The revelation of Jesus Christ which God gave
1:1-2 to Him to show to His slaves the things that must
       quickly take place; and He made *it* known by
       signs, sending *it* by His angel to His slave John,
       who testified the word of God and the testimony
       of Jesus Christ, *even* all that he saw.

6:9 And when He opened the fifth seal, I saw under-
     neath the altar the souls of those who had been
     slain because of the word of God and because of
     the testimony which they had.

We all need to enter into the depths of the book of Revelation so that we might realize that whatever we experience, enjoy, and realize of our Lord Jesus Christ is also our experience, enjoyment, and realization of the Triune God. He is revealed to such a great extent, and we must experience and enjoy Him to such an extent. Our enjoyment then becomes His testimony, and this living testimony is the present revelation of Jesus Christ. Firstly He is revealed, then we enjoy Him and become His testimony, and eventually our testimony becomes His present revelation. He is now revealed in our experience of Him as a testimony to Him. He is revealed as the all-inclusive, excellent, marvelous, mysterious, and wonderful One. We need to experience and enjoy such a Christ in so many details that our experience can become not only His testimony but also His present revelation. (*God's New Testament Economy*, pp. 235-236)

Today's Reading

In the beginning of the Bible we see God's goal in the creation of man: God wanted to have an expression of Himself. It is for this reason that man was made in the image of God. This means that man was destined to be the expression of God....The testimony of God is Jesus. This simply means that Jesus is the expression of God. God has an expression in this universe, and this expression is His testimony. Jesus, the living person expressing God Himself, is the image of God and is the testimony of God. God's intention was to have man as His expression. Adam in this respect failed God. But Jesus the second man came to replace the position of Adam and succeeded to be the testimony of God.

Jesus is the testimony of God, and the church is the testimony of Jesus. This means that the church is the expression of Jesus. In the same way that Jesus is the expression of God, the church today is the expression of Jesus. In the first two chapters of the Bible we see that man was made in the image of God to express God. In the last two chapters of the Bible there is a building called the New Jerusalem that expresses God. The book of Revelation shows that God on His throne looks like jasper (Rev. 4:3). We also see in this book that the entire New Jerusalem is in the appearance of jasper (Rev. 21:11, 18). This means that the whole city expresses God's image. Here we see the consistency of the Bible from the beginning to the end. (*The Stream,* vol. 14, no. 4, pp. 1559-1560)

Because the law is a revelation of God, it is God's testimony. According to Exodus 31:18, the two tablets of stone on which the Ten Commandments were written are called the "two tablets of the testimony." This indicates that the law was God's testimony. When the tablets of the law were put into the ark, the testimony was put in the ark....The law of the Lord is thus the testimony of the Lord. As the Lord's testimony, the law testifies of what kind of God our Lord is. Because the law, God's testimony, was placed in the ark, the ark was called the Ark of the Testimony (25:21-22; 26:33-34); and because the ark was in the tabernacle, the tabernacle was called the Tabernacle of the Testimony (38:21; Num. 1:50, 53). The law was the testimony, the ark was the Ark of the Testimony, and the tabernacle was the Tabernacle of the Testimony. (*Life-study of Exodus,* pp. 601-602)

Further Reading: God's New Testament Economy, ch. 21; The Stream, vol. 14, no. 4, part II; Life-study of Exodus, msg. 51

Enlightenment and inspiration: _____

_____

_____

_____

Morning Nourishment

Exo. **And when Moses came down from Mount Sinai...**
34:29 **Moses did not know that the skin of his face shone by reason of His speaking with him.**

Psa. **Cause Your face to shine on Your servant, and**
119:135 **teach me Your statutes.**

2 Cor. **But whenever *their heart* turns to the Lord, the**
3:16 **veil is taken away.**

18 **But we all with unveiled face, beholding and reflecting like a mirror the glory of the Lord, are being transformed into the same image from glory to glory, even as from the Lord Spirit.**

God knows how difficult it is for us to stay in His presence without doing anything. In sympathy with our weakness, He may tell us to do certain things. But it is not His intention to require us to do things. It is to keep us with Him that we may be infused with Him. But according to our natural concept, we consider that God is placing demands on us and making requirements of us. Oh, that we might see that God's intention is to infuse us with what He is and with what He has! In order for this infusion to take place, we need to be with Him.

After spending forty days on the mountaintop being infused with God, Moses was shining with God's light. Notice that God did not ask Moses to do anything. Rather, He transfused Himself into Moses until Moses began to shine with Him. This was the reason that when Moses came down from the mountain, the skin of his face was shining. The highest profession on earth is to spend time being infused with God that we may shine forth God. This is far greater than doing anything for God. If we would shine forth God, we need to spend time with Him, not to do something but to have Him transfused into our being. (*Life-study of Exodus*, p. 738)

Today's Reading

The psalmist's expression regarding the shining of the Lord's face is very sweet....We should pray, "O Lord, cause Your face to shine upon me. Lord, I long to enjoy Your shining countenance." To enjoy the shining of the Lord's face is richer and more satisfying than simply experiencing His presence.

If you are faithful in contacting the Lord through the Word, you also will experience the shining of His countenance. Your desire will be to remain under this pleasant, delightful shining. Such an experience and enjoyment prove that our God is real, present, practical, and available. What we have is not merely doctrine, but the genuine enjoyment of Him.

Some say that they find it difficult to believe in God. But because I have tasted Him and enjoy so much of Him, I find it even more difficult to deny that God exists. When I was a child, my mother loved me very much. But she could not give me the kind of enjoyment I have in the Lord. Only God Himself affords the supreme enjoyment. I do not have the words to utter how wonderful is the enjoyment of the shining of the Lord's countenance.

The law is not only a list of divine commandments; it is the living word of God which infuses God's substance into those who lovingly seek Him. If we consider the Ten Commandments only as laws and then try to keep them, we are not proper in our approach to the law. We should not apply the Ten Commandments in this way. On the contrary, we should be those who love God and seek Him. In this matter, we should be like Paul in Philippians 3, one who was pursuing Christ out of love and even running after Him. Out of love for the Lord, we should pursue Him, contact Him, and abide in His presence, dwelling together with Him. If we do this, day by day we shall be infused with God. Then automatically we shall walk according to God's law. We shall keep the requirements of the law, not by our own efforts, but with what has been infused into us of the Lord through our contact with Him. Once we have been thoroughly infused with God's substance, He Himself from within us will keep His own law. (*Life-study of Exodus,* pp. 711, 607-608)

Further Reading: Life-study of Exodus, msgs. 52, 58, 60, 62, 64

Enlightenment and inspiration: _____

_____

_____

Morning Nourishment

S. S.   **O you who dwell in the gardens, *my* companions**
8:13   **listen for your voice; let me hear *it.***
Psa.   **Your statutes have become my songs of praise**
119:54 **in the house of my pilgrimage.**
Col.   **Let the word of Christ dwell in you richly in all**
3:16   **wisdom, teaching and admonishing one an-**
            other with psalms *and* hymns *and* spiritual
            songs, singing with grace in your hearts to God.

[In Song of Songs 8:13], "you" refers to the Lord. "The gardens" are plural in number. He is not only dwelling in the garden of the maiden (6:2) but dwelling in many other gardens as well. He is the Lord who dwells in the hearts of men. He is not only dwelling in the heart of one who follows Him absolutely, but He is dwelling in the hearts of all those whom He delights in. The maiden addresses Him according to this relationship. She says to Him, "My companions listen for your voice."...All those who are seeking the Lord together with her adopt the same attitude [of listening]. They have been dealt with, and they know the futility of speaking and the profit of listening.... Those who cannot stop talking about trivial things still have the earthly life reigning within them. But these are listening; they adopt the attitude of a hearer. They know that their lives depend on the Lord's words and their work depends on the Lord's commands. They will only listen, because they cannot and will not move by themselves any longer. Without the Lord's words, they will not have any revelation, light, or knowledge. The life of the believers hinges totally upon the Lord's speaking.

"O Lord, while we are waiting to listen, make us hear. If those who seek find, and if those who knock have the door opened to them, make us hear, and make us able to hear. If Jehovah will not speak to us, we will be like those who are dead. What use is there in hearing something if it is not heard in a real way? Therefore, please allow us to hear Your voice, because only this can guide us until Your return." (W. Nee, *The Song of Songs*, pp. 124-125)

Today's Reading

Whenever we are saturated with the riches of the Word, the Word within us becomes the bountiful Spirit. This takes place through our unceasing prayer....Singing is an excellent way to pray. When you sing by exercising your spirit, you pray. Often the best prayer we can offer to God is our singing unto Him....We also pray when we thank God. When we do things in the name of the Lord Jesus, we should also give thanks to God the Father through Him.

By praying, singing, and thanking we are infused with Christ, permeated by Him, and mingled with Him. Many of us can testify that, as we were enjoying a certain portion of the Word, spontaneously a melody welled up from within. Then we began to use this melody to sing the Word to the Lord. By singing, we were saturated with the Word and nourished by its riches. This caused us to be thankful to God. At that time we were truly one with Christ. Whatever we did in word or work was done in the name of the Lord Jesus. Again I say, this is to live Christ.

The Word, the bountiful supply of the Spirit, and unceasing prayer with singing and thanking all go together. By our prayer with singing and giving thanks, the rich Word within us becomes the bountiful Spirit. Then because we are one with the Spirit, with the Word, and with Christ, we live Christ, we are truly one with Him in all we say and do. Every day we must come to the Word and allow the Word to enter into us in a rich way. For this, we need more than just the reading of the Word. We also need praying, singing, thanking, and praising. When we take the Word into us in this way, the Word becomes the Spirit with the bountiful supply. Then we are saturated with the Lord, mingled with Him, and one with Him in a practical way in life and nature. (*Life-study of Philippians,* pp. 328-329)

Further Reading: W. Nee, *The Song of Songs,* sec. 6; *Life-study of Exodus,* msg. 56; *Life-study of Philippians,* msg. 37; *Life-study of Colossians,* msg. 64

Enlightenment and inspiration: _____
_____

Morning Nourishment

Rev. And He is clothed with a garment dipped in
19:13 blood; and His name is called the Word of God.
   14 And the armies which are in heaven followed
      Him on white horses, dressed in fine linen, white
      and clean.
   15 And out of His mouth proceeds a sharp sword,
      that with it He might smite the nations; and He
      will shepherd them with an iron rod; and He
      treads the winepress of the fury of the wrath of
      God the Almighty.

[In Revelation 19:15], the sword, which proceeds out of the mouth of Christ, who is the Word of God, is the word which will judge the rebellious (John 12:48). When the Lord Jesus comes to fight against Antichrist, He will not need nuclear weapons. He will simply need to speak a word. If He were to say, "Antichrist, go to the lake of fire," Antichrist would immediately be cast there. The Lord's word is more powerful than a nuclear weapon. As the Lord is speaking, we who follow Him shall say, "Amen." When the Lord says, "Antichrist, go to the lake of fire," we all shall say, "Amen," and Antichrist will immediately be cast into the lake of fire. This is the Lord's way of fighting. Undoubtedly, Antichrist will use the most modern weapons, but Christ will defeat him with the sharp sword, the almighty word that proceeds out of His mouth. (*Life-study of Revelation,* pp. 638-639)

Today's Reading

In Revelation 19:11-21 we see that the Bridegroom comes to fight against His enemies with the help of His bride. The Bridegroom is the Commander-in-chief, and the bride is the army. What a honeymoon this will be! During His honeymoon Christ will clear up the universe. Antichrist and the false prophet will be cast into the lake of fire, and Satan will be bound and cast into the abyss. At that time Christ will be happy, and we, His bride, shall also be happy as we enjoy a wonderful honeymoon with our Bridegroom.

Verse 13 also says, "His name is called the Word of God." The Word of God is the definition, the explanation, and the expression of God. As the Word of God, Christ speaks for God not only by imparting life as grace to God's chosen people in the Gospel of John (John 1:1, 4, 14), but also by executing God's judgment upon the rebellious people in the Revelation of John. Even as the Lord fights, He speaks for God and expresses God. The fighting of Christ is the speaking of the Word of God. God is righteous and sovereign. He is also a God of order and He cannot tolerate disorder and rebellion. As Christ fights against the enemy, He will speak that God is sovereign, righteous, and orderly. He will declare that God is the God over everyone and that He does not tolerate rebellion against His authority. Hence, the Warrior is the Word. His fighting is the speaking of God's Word.

The Lord's fighting in the war at Armageddon will be a powerful speaking. It will tell Satan, Antichrist, the false prophet, and the entire universe that God is sovereign and that no one can rebel against Him. God is a God of order and He will sweep away all rebellion.

The Word of God is mentioned both in the Gospel of John (1:1) and in the Revelation of John. In the Gospel of John the Word of God does not speak anything related to fighting; rather, He speaks redemption, light, life, and building. In the Gospel of John the Word of God speaks life and building. In the Revelation of John the Word of God speaks not only life and building, but also fighting. Before God can have the building He desires, He must first clean up His universe. In this book Christ's fighting is also His speaking for God. As the Word of God, His fighting proclaims to the whole universe what kind of God He is. God is not a God of confusion—He is the sovereign God, a God of order who does not tolerate rebellion. By His fighting Christ declares this to the universe. *(Life-study of Revelation,* pp. 633, 637-638)

Further Reading: Life-study of Revelation, msg. 55

Enlightenment and inspiration: _____

_____

_____

Morning Nourishment

Eph. And receive the helmet of salvation and the sword
6:17 of the Spirit, which *Spirit* is the word of God.
Heb. For the word of God is living and operative and
4:12 sharper than any two-edged sword, and piercing
even to the dividing of soul and spirit and of
joints and marrow, and able to discern the
thoughts and intentions of the heart.

Because the self is the greatest enemy, we need to experience the killing power of God's word. As we pray-read, we are nourished on the one hand, but certain elements are killed on the other hand. Perhaps you are troubled by doubts, hatred, jealousy, pride, or selfishness. Do you realize that these things can be killed through pray-reading the word? The more we take in the word with its killing power, the more our pride and all the negative elements within us are put to death. By pray-reading, the inward adversary is slain. After a time of pray-reading the word, we may discover that the adversary who was attacking us has disappeared. In a very practical sense, he has been slain by the word we have taken into us.

Do not think that the battlefield for the spiritual warfare is outside us. The battlefield is within us; in particular it is in our mind. All the elements of the adversary can be found in the mind. The way to slay them is to pray-read the word. As we pray-read God's word, the elements of the adversary within our mind will be killed one by one. In this way we shall gain the victory. (*Life-study of Ephesians*, pp. 820-821)

Today's Reading

This is something I have learned through many years of experience. I am not a "marble" person who cannot be offended. I have often been offended by others in the church life or in my family life. How have I been able to get through all the offenses? I get through by receiving the word as the Spirit. The word I receive as the Spirit then becomes the sword to slay the enemy.

Apparently the sword of the Spirit kills my emotion; actually it kills the evil spirit in the air who takes advantage of my emotion. Whereas my emotion is killed directly, the evil spirit is killed indirectly. In this way I have been able to get through the offenses.

When some hear this they might say, "Brother Lee, show me a verse that can kill your emotion directly and kill the evil power in the air indirectly." This is not a matter of a particular verse that touches our emotion but a matter of applying Ephesians 6:17 in an experiential way. Suppose in the evening I am offended by one of the elders. Because I fear the Lord, I do not dare to talk about this with others. The next morning I rise up to contact the Lord in the Word. I do not read any verses that touch the matter of my emotion. Instead, I simply begin to read the Bible with the exercise of the spirit. I may read Genesis 1:1: "In the beginning God created the heavens and the earth." As I read this verse, I receive the word in a living way as the Spirit, and the Spirit, which is the word, becomes the sword that kills my emotion directly and kills the evil force indirectly. Spontaneously, the offense is gone, and no damage is done to the church. However, if the offense were allowed to remain, it would cause serious damage to the church life. I believe that many of us have experienced receiving the word of God in this way.

Without the word as the Spirit to be the killing sword, there would be no way for us to be kept in the church life over the years. For more than half a century, I have been traveling, visiting the churches, and contacting thousands of saints. Without the word as the Spirit to kill all the enemies, I would not still be here ministering. If I had allowed myself to remain offended with a certain church or saint, I would have been finished with the ministry. I have been kept in the church life and in the ministry through the killing of the word as the Spirit. (*Teachers' Training*, pp. 22-23)

Further Reading: Life-study of Ephesians, msg. 97; Teachers' Training, ch. 2

Enlightenment and inspiration: _____

_____

Morning Nourishment

Rev. And she brought forth a son, a man-child, who is
12:5 to shepherd all the nations with an iron rod; and
her child was caught up to God and to His throne.

19:7 Let us rejoice and exult, and let us give the glory
to Him, for the marriage of the Lamb has come,
and His wife has made herself ready.

10 ...I am your fellow slave and *a fellow slave* of your
brothers who have the testimony of Jesus. Worship God. For the testimony of Jesus is the spirit
of the prophecy.

In Revelation 19:7-9 we see the church as the bride. Ephesians 5 reveals that the church is the bride of Christ, but it does
not reveal the bride in such an intimate way. But in Revelation 19
we see how intimate is the church as the bride. In this portion
of the Word we see that the bride will wear bright raiment, being
clothed with bright and pure righteousness, and will be invited
to the marriage feast of the Lamb (vv. 7-9). This is a very
intimate matter. To God's enemy, we must be the man-child; for
God's satisfaction, we must be the firstfruits; and for Christ, we
must be the bride. When we are eager to be the bride, Christ will
receive His satisfaction. Not only will Christ be satisfied, but
we ourselves will be glad....The day is coming when there will
be no more persecutions, sufferings, or dealings....Oh, we must
be the bride! When we have become the bride, all the difficult
dealings will be over. (*Life-study of Revelation,* pp. 35-36)

Today's Reading

The testimony of Jesus is the spirit—the reality, the substance, the disposition, and the characteristic—of the prophecy
in the book of Revelation (Rev. 19:10b). The entire book of
Revelation is a prophecy of Jesus, and the reality of this prophecy is the testimony of Jesus. This reality is the spirit. This is
like saying that the orange juice is the spirit of the orange. We
may also say that the spirit, the reality, of the entire Bible is the

testimony of Jesus. (*1993 Blending Conference Messages concerning the Lord's Recovery and Our Present Need,* p. 100)

As we have seen, the man-child is the stronger part of the people of God. Among the people of God, even among us in the Lord's recovery today, there is the stronger part. This stronger part will be raptured to the throne of God before the great tribulation. In other words, the woman will be left on earth to pass through the tribulation, but the stronger part, the man-child, will be raptured to the throne of God before the tribulation. Why will the man-child be raptured prior to the tribulation? Because God needs the man-child to fight Satan in the heavens and to cast him down. Although God has many angels who will fight against Satan, the final victory over the enemy will not be gained by the angels but by the man-child. God needs the man-child. God will shame Satan by using the very man Satan corrupted to defeat him....The man-child will fight through and up, fighting up to the throne to cast Satan down from the heavens to the earth. This is a part of the testimony of Jesus. Although Jesus has defeated Satan on the cross, there is still the need for the church to execute His victory over the enemy. Because so many members of the Body have failed in this matter, only the stronger part of the Body, the man-child, will execute Christ's victory over Satan. The man-child will be raptured to the heavens to accomplish this job.

Ultimately, the testimony of Jesus will be the New Jerusalem (21:1—22:5). Beginning with the lampstand and passing through the great multitude, the man-child, the firstfruits, the late overcomers, the bride, and the army, all the saved ones will eventually be the New Jerusalem, which will be a living composition of all of God's redeemed ones, the ultimate consummation of God's building of His people. In and for eternity, the New Jerusalem will express God in the Lamb with the flow of the Spirit. (*Life-study of Revelation,* pp. 31-32, 36)

Further Reading: Life-study of Revelation, msg. 3; *1993 Blending Conference Messages concerning the Lord's Recovery and Our Present Need,* msg. 5

Enlightenment and inspiration: _____

_____

Hymns, #1226

1 Oh, the church of Christ is glorious, and we are part of it—
  We're so happy that the Lord has made us one!
There's a Body in the universe and we belong to it—
  Hallelujah, for the Lord has made us one!

> Hallelujah for the Body!
> We are members of the Body!
> We are wholly for the Body!
> Hallelujah, for the Lord has made us one!

2 Not the individual Christians, but a corporate entity—
  God must have it for His full expression now;
Not just individual churches but the Body corporately—
  Hallelujah, we are in the Body now!

> Hallelujah for the Body!
> Satan trembles at the Body!
> We're victorious in the Body!
> Hallelujah, we are in the Body now!

3 There are seven golden lampstands in the nature all divine—
  Nothing natural does the Body life allow.
When we're one and share God's nature, how the lampstand
  then does shine—
  Hallelujah, it is brightly shining now!

> Hallelujah for the Body!
> For the lampstands of the Body!
> For the golden, shining Body!
> Hallelujah, it is brightly shining now!

4 How may we express such oneness, be divine and
  shining too?
  Hallelujah, eating Jesus is the way!
He's the tree of life, the manna, and the feast that's
  ever new—
  Hallelujah, we may eat Him every day!

> We are one by eating Jesus!
> We're divine by eating Jesus!
> How we shine by eating Jesus!
> Hallelujah, eating Jesus is the way!

Composition for prophecy with main point and sub-points: _____

_____
_____
_____
_____
_____
_____
_____
_____
_____
_____
_____
_____
_____
_____
_____
_____
_____
_____
_____
_____
_____
_____
_____
_____
_____
_____
_____
_____
_____
_____
_____
_____
_____
_____
_____
_____

The Triune God and the Divine Trinity

Scripture Reading: Rev. 1:4-5; 22:17a; 4:5; 5:6

Day 1
  I. The Triune God mainly refers to God Himself, the divine Person; the Divine Trinity mainly refers to God's being triune, which is the primary attribute of the Godhead (Matt. 28:19; Rev. 1:4-5).

Day 2
  II. The Trinity in Revelation is the economical Trinity (1:4-5):

    A. The essential Trinity refers to the essence of the Triune God for His existence; the economical Trinity refers to God's plan for His move (Matt. 28:19; Rev. 1:4-5):

      1. In the essential Trinity the Father, the Son, and the Spirit coexist and coinhere at the same time and in the same way with no succession.

      2. In the economical Trinity the Father, the Son, and the Spirit work in three successive steps, or stages, in the process of God's economy:

        a. The Father planned, the Son accomplished, and the Spirit applies what the Son accomplished according to the Father's plan (Eph. 1:4-5, 7, 13).

        b. While the divine economy is being carried out, the eternal coexistence and coinherence of the three in the Godhead remain intact and are not jeopardized.

    B. The Trinity in Matthew 28:19 is the Trinity of God's existence—the essential Trinity—but the Trinity in Revelation 1:4-5 is the Trinity in God's economy—the economical Trinity:

      1. In Revelation we see the administration, the government, the activity, the move, the act, and the work of the Trinity (4:5; 5:6).

    2. In God's essence the Trinity is simply the Father, the Son, and the Spirit, but in God's economy the Trinity is complicated:

      a. The Father is the One "who is and who was and who is coming" (1:4b).

      b. The Spirit is "the seven Spirits who are before His throne" (v. 4c).

      c. The Son is "Jesus Christ, the faithful Witness, the Firstborn of the dead, and the Ruler of the kings of the earth" (v. 5a).

Day 3 **III. The Triune God in Revelation is the processed and consummated Triune God (22:17a; 3:22; 14:13):**

A. The God in Genesis 1 is the unprocessed God, but the God in Revelation is the processed and consummated Triune God:

    1. *Processed* refers to the crucial steps through which the Triune God has passed in the divine economy, and *consummated* indicates that the process has been completed.

    2. Before His incarnation God was unprocessed, having the divine nature but not the human nature, but through incarnation, human living, crucifixion, resurrection, and ascension, the Triune God was processed and consummated.

    3. In Revelation the Triune God is the processed and consummated Triune God with divinity, humanity, human living, the all-inclusive death, the powerful resurrection, and the transcendent ascension (1:4-5).

B. The processed and consummated Triune God is *the Spirit* (Rev. 22:17a; John 7:39):

    1. The Spirit is the totality, the aggregate, of all the elements of the titles of the Spirit of God (Luke 1:35; Matt. 3:16; 10:20; Luke

4:18; Gal. 4:6; Acts 16:7; Rom. 8:9; Phil. 1:19).

2. As the consummation of the processed and consummated Triune God, the Spirit is the blessing of God's New Testament economy (Gal. 3:14).

Day 4 IV. **The Triune God in Revelation is the sevenfold intensified Spirit (3:1; 4:5; 5:6):**

A. Because of the degradation of the church, the Spirit has been intensified sevenfold to become the sevenfold intensified Spirit (1:4).

B. The sevenfold intensified Spirit intensifies all the elements of the Spirit (3:1).

C. The sevenfold intensified Spirit is for God's move to carry out His administration (4:5; 5:6).

Day 5 V. **The Triune God in Revelation is the building and builded God (21:18-19a, 21a):**

A. The Bible consummates in the New Jerusalem, which is the very God who was in the beginning (Gen. 1:1; Rev. 21:2, 10):

1. The unique God is eventually enlarged and expanded into a city for His eternal expression (Gen. 1:1; Rev. 21:2).

2. In His economy God has become the New Jerusalem (21:10).

3. The New Jerusalem is the Triune God wrought into His redeemed (21:18-19a, 21).

B. The God who has become the New Jerusalem is the building and builded God (2 Sam. 7:12-14a; Matt. 16:18; Eph. 3:17):

1. The processed and consummated Triune God as the source, the element, and the essence is building the church by building Himself into our being (Eph. 3:17).

2. God is fulfilling His desire to build Himself in Christ into our being and to build us into His being; eventually, the outcome of this

building will be the New Jerusalem (Rev. 21:2, 10).

Day 6 **VI. In the book of Revelation, we have the consummate revelation of the Divine Trinity for the divine dispensing (2 Cor. 13:14; Rev. 22:1-2; 7:17a; 21:6b; John 4:14b):**

A. The divine dispensing is God's imparting of Himself into His chosen and redeemed people as their life, their life supply, and their everything (2 Cor. 13:14).

B. In the divine dispensing, the Father is the fountain, the Son is the spring, and the Spirit is the flow (Jer. 2:13; John 4:10, 14; 7:37-39; Rev. 22:1; 7:17a; 21:6b):

1. As the origin the Father is the fountain of living waters (Jer. 2:13).

2. As the embodiment and expression of the Father, the Son is the spring, the emergence of the fountain (John 4:14).

3. As the transmission the Spirit is the river (Rev. 22:1).

4. This is the Divine Trinity in the divine dispensing—God the Father as the source, God the Son as the course, and God the Spirit as the flow.

Morning Nourishment

**Matt. Go therefore and disciple all the nations, bap-
28:19 tizing them into the name of the Father and of
the Son and of the Holy Spirit.**

In 1977 I visited Israel with a group of brothers. One day we went to the source of the Jordan River at the foot of Mount Hermon. There is a spring there with a fountain as the source. The spring has a flow, and the flow is a stream, a river. Such a river is a picture of our Triune God with the Father as the source, the Son as the course, and the Spirit as the flow. This is the biblical illustration in Revelation 22.

In Revelation 22:1 the Son is the Lamb, indicating that the Son is the Redeemer. The river of water of life proceeds out of the throne of God and of the Lamb....God is in the Lamb on the throne, and out of His throne flows the river of water of life, the Spirit. When the Spirit flows it carries the Lamb. Then in the flow of the river, the Lamb becomes the tree of life (Rev. 22:2). The tree of life growing on the two sides of the river signifies that the tree of life is a vine, spreading and proceeding along the flow of the water of life for God's people to receive and enjoy. The tree of life symbolizes the Triune God to be our life supply. The Triune God is the water of life for us to drink and the tree of life for us to eat. (*The Central Line of the Divine Revelation*, pp. 22-23)

Today's Reading

We need to go on to see the difference between the Triune God and the Divine Trinity. The Triune God mainly refers to God Himself, and the Divine Trinity mainly refers to God's being triune, which is the main attribute of the Godhead. It is more correct to refer the divine dispensing to the Divine Trinity rather than to the Triune God. The Triune God refers to God the Person, while the Divine Trinity refers to the main attribute of the Godhead. For example, saying that someone is a faithful person is different from saying that he is faithfulness.

A faithful person refers to the man. His faithfulness refers to his being faithful, his virtue. In a general way God is dispensing Himself into us, but in a particular, actual, and practical way God is dispensing His Trinity into us.

The Divine Trinity is the top divine attribute of our God. In the theological study of the past concerning God's person, the word *triune* was invented. *Triune* is an adjective just as *holy* is an adjective. The Triune God bears an attribute which is trinity. Just as holy produces holiness so triune produces trinity. Holiness is an attribute of God and trinity is also an attribute of God. In 2 Corinthians 13:14 grace, love, and fellowship are attributes of the Triune God, but the top attribute of our God is the Trinity. To say that He is dispensing Himself into us is a general speaking. Specifically speaking, we must realize that He is dispensing His Trinity because His Trinity is the top and all-inclusive attribute including His love, His grace, His fellowship, His holiness, and His everything.

If God were not triune, the Father, the Son, and the Spirit, He could not have a way to dispense Himself into us. Many works have been accomplished in God's economy, which consists of three steps, and this economy is the economy of the very one God who is essentially one. He performed many works. The Father exercised His foreknowledge. He chose us and predestinated us in the Son and with the Spirit. As the Son, the Triune God did many works in creation, incarnation, human living, crucifixion, resurrection, and ascension. Now He is doing a finer work as the Spirit in regeneration, sanctification, transformation, conformation, and glorification. He is also living in us and guiding us in many, many things as the Spirit. (*Elders' Training, Book 3: The Way to Carry Out the Vision,* pp. 71, 83-84)

Further Reading: The Central Line of the Divine Revelation, msg. 2; *Elders' Training, Book 3: The Way to Carry Out the Vision,* chs. 7-8

Enlightenment and inspiration: _____

_____

_____

Morning Nourishment

Rev.   ...Grace to you and peace from Him who is and
1:4-5   who was and who is coming, and from the seven
        Spirits who are before His throne, and from Jesus
        Christ, the faithful Witness, the Firstborn of the
        dead, and the Ruler of the kings of the earth....
Eph.   Even as He chose us in Him,...predestinating us
1:4-5   unto sonship through Jesus Christ to Himself,
        according to the good pleasure of His will.
   7   In whom we have redemption....
  13   ...In Him also believing, you were sealed with the
        Holy Spirit of the promise.

[In Revelation 1:4-5], the first of the Trinity was moving
in the past, is moving in the present, and is going to move
in the future. This is economical. The second of the Trinity
is the seven Spirits before the administrative throne of
God. This is also economical. Finally, all the points concerning the Son as Jesus Christ, the Witness, the Firstborn of
the dead, and the Ruler of the kings of the earth, do not
refer to His essence but to His move and His activity. The
Triune God became Jesus, and Jesus was anointed to be
the Christ. Jesus Christ was the faithful Witness on this
earth who died and was resurrected to be the Firstborn of
God to produce many brothers that the church might be
brought forth. Now He is the Ruler of the kings of the earth,
He has accomplished redemption for us, and He has made
us a kingdom, even the priesthood to His God and Father.
Also, He will come again. All these points indicate His move
and His economy. (*God's New Testament Economy*, p. 232)

Today's Reading

It is evident, therefore, that the divine revelation of the
Trinity of the Godhead in the holy Word, from Genesis
through Revelation, is not for the study of theology, but for
the understanding of how God in His mysterious and

marvelous trinity dispenses Himself into His chosen people so that we, as His chosen and redeemed people, may, as indicated in Paul's blessing to the Corinthian believers in 2 Corinthians 13:14, participate in, experience, enjoy, and possess the processed Triune God now and for eternity. (*Life-study of the New Testament, Conclusion Messages,* p. 27)

The essential Trinity refers to the essence of the Triune God for His existence. In His essence, God is one, the one unique God (Isa. 45:18b; 1 Cor. 8:6a). In the essential Trinity, the Father, the Son, and the Spirit coexist and coinhere at the same time and in the same way with no succession. There is no first, second, or third.

Essentially, God is one, but economically He is three—the Father, the Son, and the Spirit (Matt. 28:19; 2 Cor. 13:14). In God's plan, God's administrative arrangement, God's economy, the Father takes the first step, the Son takes the second step, and the Spirit takes the third step. The Father purposed (Eph. 1:4-6), the Son accomplished (vv. 7-12), and the Spirit applies what the Son accomplished according to the Father's purpose (vv. 13-14). This is a successive procedure or a succession in God's economy to carry out His eternal purpose. Whereas the essential Trinity refers to the essence of the Triune God for His existence, the economical Trinity refers to His plan for His move. There is the need of the existence of the Divine Trinity, and there is also the need of the plan of the Divine Trinity. (*The Crucial Points of the Major Items of the Lord's Recovery Today,* pp. 9-10)

Further Reading: Life-study of the New Testament, Conclusion Messages, msgs. 3, 6; God's New Testament Economy, chs. 20-21; The Crucial Points of the Major Items of the Lord's Recovery Today; Living in and with the Divine Trinity, ch. 6

Enlightenment and inspiration: _____

_____

_____

_____

process — The step The Lord had to go to
Consummated — the completion
WEEK 3 — DAY 3   **46**

Morning Nourishment

**Rev. 22:17 And the Spirit and the bride say, Come!...
3:22 He who has an ear, let him hear what the
Spirit says to the churches.**

Today many Christians have never heard of the processed
and consummated God. Hence, what they are preaching is
the unprocessed God in Genesis chapter one. However, what
we have seen is the consummated God in Revelation chapter
twenty-two. At the end the Bible says, "The Spirit and the
bride say..." (Rev. 22:17). The Spirit is the processed and
consummated God; the bride is the processed and consummated church. The two are joined to be a loving pair in
eternity. The final word of the Bible is the highest authority
for defining the truth. The Lord in His recovery has already
shown us the highest truth defined by the Bible. (*The Issue
of the Union of the Consummated Spirit of the Triune God
and the Regenerated Spirit of the Believers,* p. 77)

Today's Reading

Before His process in eternity past (John 1:1), God was
"raw," having only divinity. Through incarnation, the first
step of His process, humanity was added to Him. After
incarnation He is of two elements, divinity and humanity. Then He went to the cross and went through an all-
inclusive death. The element of His death was then added
to Him. Three days after His crucifixion, He entered into
resurrection; thus, another element, resurrection, was also
added to Him. Divinity, humanity, crucifixion, and resurrection all are the elements of the processed Triune God.
As the "raw God," He was life only to Himself, but as the
processed God, the "cooked God," He can be life to us. In
resurrection He is the consummated Spirit, the consummation of the processed God to be life to us. This Spirit is called
the Spirit of life [Rom. 8:2].

Today the God we love and whom we have received is

not the "raw" God, but the "cooked" God. The cooked God today is Jesus Christ, and Jesus Christ is the consummated Spirit to be life and everything to His believers (1 Cor. 15:45b). (*The Experience and Growth in Life,* pp. 56, 136)

Some find fault with the word *processed* and argue that it is impossible for God to be processed because He is eternal and unchanging. Although God is eternal and unchanging, He has nevertheless passed through a process. (*Life-study of Galatians,* p. 290)

At the end of the Bible, Revelation 22:17 refers to "the Spirit." This verse mentions the Spirit and the bride. The Spirit is the consummation of the processed Triune God, and the bride is the consummation of the transformed, tripartite man. The processed God marries the transformed man. The Husband is triune, and the wife is tripartite. They match each other. The Triune God has been processed, and the tripartite man will have been transformed. God was processed by putting on man's nature, and man was transformed by partaking of God's nature. God took man's nature to get processed, and man took God's nature to get transformed. Man and God are married in their nature. God's nature becomes man's nature; man's nature becomes God's nature. The conclusion of the entire sixty-six books of the Bible is the marriage of a couple. This couple is the processed Triune God and the transformed tripartite man. (*The Spirit,* pp. 28-29)

Further Reading: The Issue of the Union of the Consummated Spirit of the Triune God and the Regenerated Spirit of the Believers, ch. 6; The Experience and Growth in Life, msgs. 9, 11, 20; The Governing and Controlling Vision in the Bible, ch. 3; Life-study of Galatians, msgs. 33, 38; The Triune God to Be Life to the Tripartite Man, msgs. 5-6; Life-study of the New Testament, Conclusion Messages, msg. 80; The Divine Dispensing of the Divine Trinity, ch. 14; The Spirit, ch. 2

Enlightenment and inspiration: _____

_____

_____

Morning Nourishment

Rev. ...These things says He who has the seven Spirits
3:1 of God....
4:5 ...And *there were* seven lamps of fire burning before
the throne, which are the seven Spirits of God.
5:6 And I saw...a Lamb standing as having *just* been
slain, having seven horns and seven eyes, which are
the seven Spirits of God sent forth into all the earth.

The seven Spirits of God burning before God's throne as a flame of fire are judging the entire world, both the believers and the unbelievers. According to 1 Peter 4:17 this judgment begins from the house of God and will spread to the unbelievers, the entire earth. The seven Spirits are sent forth unto all the earth to judge the earth, to purify the earth, to refine the earth, and to bring forth the pure golden lampstands, shining in this dark age as the testimony of Jesus....Many Christians and all the people of the world do not know what is going on behind the scenes in today's world situation. We realize, however, according to His enlightening Word, that the seven Spirits today are burning to judge, to purify, and to refine with a purpose. The burning of the seven Spirits of God before God's administrative throne has a purpose to bring forth the golden lampstands, the churches, for the fulfillment of God's New Testament economy. (*God's New Testament Economy*, pp. 249-250)

Today's Reading

In the book of Revelation the Spirit is called the seven Spirits (1:4; 4:5; 5:6), the sevenfold intensified Spirit to counteract the degradation of the church. The seven Spirits in Revelation 1:4 undoubtedly are the Spirit of God because They are ranked among the Triune God. As seven is the number for completion in God's operation, so the seven Spirits must be for God's move on earth. In substance and existence God's Spirit is one. In the intensified function and work of God's operation His Spirit is sevenfold. It is like the lampstand in Zechariah 4:2. In existence it is one lampstand, but in function it is seven lamps. At the time the book of Revelation was written, the church had become degraded, and the age was dark. Therefore, the sevenfold intensified Spirit of God was needed for God's move on earth.

The seven lamps here refer to the seven lamps of the lampstand in Exodus 25:37 and...in Zechariah 4:2. The seven lamps of fire which are the seven Spirits of God signify the enlightening and searching of the sevenfold intensified Spirit of God. In Exodus 25 and Zechariah 4 the seven lamps, signifying the enlightening of the Spirit of God in God's move, are for God's building, either for the tabernacle or the rebuilding of the temple. Here the seven lamps are for God's judgment, which will issue also in God's building—the building of the New Jerusalem.

Eyes are for observing and searching. Christ as the redeeming Lamb has seven observing and searching eyes for executing God's judgment upon the universe to fulfill God's eternal purpose, which will consummate in the building up of the New Jerusalem. Therefore, in Zechariah 3:9 He is prophesied as the stone, which is the topstone (Zech. 4:7), with seven eyes for God's building. These seven eyes are the seven Spirits of God sent forth into all the earth, running "to and fro on the whole earth" (Zech. 4:10).

The seven Spirits as the seven eyes of the Lamb are also for transfusing. When Christ looks at us with His seven eyes, these eyes, which are the seven Spirits, will transfuse Christ's element into us. Whereas the seven Spirits as the seven lamps of burning fire are for enlightening and burning, the seven Spirits as the seven eyes of the Lamb are for observing, searching, and transfusing. As the Lord enlightens and judges us, He looks at us, and through the seven Spirits as His eyes He transfuses Himself into us for our transformation. (*Life-study of the New Testament, Conclusion Messages,* pp. 867-868)

Further Reading: God's New Testament Economy, ch. 22; *Life-study of the New Testament, Conclusion Messages,* msg. 80; *The Divine Economy,* ch. 14; *The Spirit,* ch. 2; *The Spirit with Our Spirit,* ch. 7

Enlightenment and inspiration: _____

Morning Nourishment

Rev. **And the building work of its wall was jasper;**
21:18 **and the city was pure gold, like clear glass.**
  19 **The foundations of the wall of the city were**
      adorned with every precious stone....
  21 **And the twelve gates were twelve pearls....**

Our work in the recovery today is to minister God to people. Yes, we need to save sinners and to feed the saints and perfect them. The crucial matter, however, is that we minister God to others. The God whom we minister is not just the building God—He is also the builded God. If we fail to minister God in this way, our work will be wood, grass, and stubble (1 Cor. 3:12).

I would ask you to reconsider the work you are doing for the Lord....How much of Christ as the embodiment of the Triune God has been wrought into those whom you have brought to God? If we are sincere and genuine, we will humble ourselves and confess that not very much of the Triune God has been wrought into the ones we have brought to God. Therefore, we need to practice one thing—to minister the processed Triune God into others so that He may build Himself into their inner man. In every aspect of our work—preaching the gospel, feeding the believers, perfecting the saints—the intrinsic element must be that we minister the building and builded God to others. I would urge you to pray that the Lord would teach you to work in this way. (*Life-study of 1 & 2 Samuel*, p. 201)

Today's Reading

God in Christ is constituting Himself into man, making Himself the element of man. Thus, we human beings are constituted with a divine element. This means that a divine element is built into our human element, and the two elements are mingled with each other. Not only is God's divine element constituted into us—the human element is constituted into God. As the divine element is constituted into our humanity, we become God in life and in nature but not in the Godhead. As the human element is constituted into God, God becomes man. This is the building revealed in the New Testament.

Such a revelation should become a principle that governs our understanding of God and of God's building. When we talk about the building up of the church or about the building up of the Body, we need to realize that this building is a constitution of the divine element into the human element and of the human element into the divine element,...a constitution of the divine element and of the human element into each other. Such a constitution makes the divine element and the human element one entity. This is the building of the church, the building of the Body of Christ.

The New Jerusalem is a composition of divinity and humanity blended and mingled together as one entity. All the components have the same life, nature, and constitution and thus are a corporate person. This is a matter of God becoming man and man becoming God in life and in nature but not in the Godhead. These two, God and man, man and God, are built up together by being blended and mingled together. This is the completion, the consummation, of God's building. We all need to see this vision. (*Life-study of 1 & 2 Samuel*, pp. 205-206, 199)

Our God is the processed and consummated Triune God, and we are the redeemed, regenerated, transformed, conformed, glorified tripartite man. He mingles with us, and we mingle with Him to be one. The New Jerusalem is not merely God or merely man. The New Jerusalem is a God-man in the corporate way. The New Jerusalem is a mingling of the processed, consummated Triune God with the redeemed, regenerated, transformed, conformed, and glorified tripartite man. He is triune, we are tripartite, and we are mingled with Him. (*The Central Line of the Divine Revelation*, p. 331)

Further Reading: Life-study of 1 & 2 Samuel, msgs. 30-31; *The Central Line of the Divine Revelation*, msg. 28; *Crystallization-study of the Gospel of John*, msg. 16; *God's New Testament Economy*, ch. 22; *The Issue of Christ Being Glorified by the Father with the Divine Glory*, ch. 5; *A Word of Love to the Co-workers, Elders, Lovers, and Seekers of the Lord*, ch. 2

Enlightenment and inspiration: _____

_____

Morning Nourishment

John   But whoever drinks of the water that I will give
4:14   him shall by no means thirst forever; but the
       water that I will give him will become in him a
       fountain of water gushing up into eternal life.
Rev.   For the Lamb who is in the midst of the throne
7:17   will shepherd them and guide them to springs
       of waters of life....
21:6   ...I will give to him who thirsts from the spring
       of the water of life freely.

The first four chapters [of the Gospel of John] unveil the
flowing God in His divine processed Trinity. In John
4:14b,...God the Father is the fountain emerging in God the Son
as a spring gushing up to be a river, signifying God the Spirit.
The Triune God flows into eternal life, and the eternal life has
its totality. Our human life also has its totality. A living person
is the totality of the human life. The totality of the divine life is
the New Jerusalem, which is the destination of the flowing
Triune God. (*Crystallization-study of the Gospel of John*, p. 143)

Today's Reading

The goal of having the divine life is the New Jerusalem. God
loved the human race [John 3:16], the worst human people, with
the intention that they all may participate in the New Jerusalem....To have eternal life means to be joined to, to participate
in, the New Jerusalem. The banners for the *Crystallization-
study of the Gospel of John* say that the Triune God who passed
through all the processes, the all-inclusive Christ who was
incarnated to die and resurrect, and the life-giving Spirit who
was consummated to indwell us all take the New Jerusalem as
Their eternal goal....In this crystallization-study I thoroughly
and intrinsically came to the clear conclusion that this Gospel,
especially from chapter one to chapter four, is the record of the
flowing God in His three stages: the Father as the fountain, the
Son as the spring, and the Spirit as the flowing river. Moreover,

They all take the New Jerusalem as Their eternal goal. Apparently, the New Jerusalem is not mentioned in John. However, it is seen in the eternal life in 4:14. *Eternal life* here is the totality of the divine life. A man is the totality of the human life; each one of us is the totality of the human life, but the divine life has only one totality in the whole universe—the New Jerusalem.

The Bible teaches us that eternal life is God Himself. In the beginning there is God as the eternal life, and the consummation of God as the eternal life is the New Jerusalem. The Bible consummates in the New Jerusalem, which is the very God who was in the beginning. How does God become the New Jerusalem? It is through His flowing. The Bible has two ends, Genesis 1—2 and Revelation 21—22. At the beginning of the Bible there is God, at the end there is the New Jerusalem, and in between are hundreds of pages speaking about all the matters related to the eternal life, including the believers, regeneration, transformation, conformation, and glorification. This is the proper way to view the Bible. All the activities of the eternal life take the New Jerusalem as the final goal. This is the meaning of "into eternal life" in John 4:14. The word *into* is also used in 1 Corinthians 12:13, which says that the Gentiles and the Jews have all been baptized in one Spirit into one Body. *Into one Body* does not mean merely to enter into the Body but to become the Body. In the same way, *into eternal life* does not merely mean to enter into the New Jerusalem as the eternal life but to become the New Jerusalem as the eternal life. The coming New Jerusalem will be you and me. We are the New Jerusalem. The New Jerusalem is still under a consummating work, and this consummating work is the flow of the divine life. This is very deep. (*A Word of Love to the Co-workers, Elders, Lovers, and Seekers of the Lord,* pp. 23-24)

Further Reading: Crystallization-study of the Gospel of John, msg. 15; *A Word of Love to the Co-workers, Elders, Lovers, and Seekers of the Lord,* ch. 2; *Life-study of 1 John,* msg. 32; *The Stream,* vol. 14, no. 3, part VII

Enlightenment and inspiration: _____

_____

_____

Hymns, #608

1   What mystery, the Father, Son, and Spirit,
      In person three, in substance all are one.
    How glorious, this God our being enters
      To be our all, thru Spirit in the Son!

      The Triune God has now become our all!
        How wonderful! How glorious!
      This Gift divine we never can exhaust!
        How excellent! How marvelous!

2   How rich the source, the Father as the fountain,
      And all this wealth He wants man to enjoy!
    O blessed fact, this vast exhaustless portion
      Is now for us forever to employ!

3   How wonderful, the Son is God's expression
      Come in the flesh to dwell with all mankind!
    Redemption's work, how perfectly effective,
      That sinners we with God might oneness find.

4   The Spirit is the Son's transfiguration
      Come into us as life the full supply.
    Amazing fact, our spirit with the Spirit
      Now mingles and in oneness joins thereby!

5   How real it is that God is now the Spirit
      For us to touch, experience day by day!
    Astounding fact, with God we are one spirit,
      And differ not in life in any way!

Composition for prophecy with main point and sub-points: _____

_____
_____
_____
_____
_____
_____
_____
_____
_____
_____
_____
_____
_____
_____
_____
_____
_____
_____
_____
_____
_____
_____
_____
_____
_____
_____
_____
_____
_____
_____
_____
_____
_____

*The Revelation of Christ in His Coming Back
and the Prophecy of the Four "Sevens"
concerning the Consummation of the Age*

Scripture Reading: Rev. 1:7; 3:3; 16:15; 10:1; 18:1; 19:7-9a, 19-20

Day 1

I. **We need to see the full revelation of Christ in His coming back (1:7):**

A. The revelation of the person of Christ in His coming back:

1. In His coming back Christ will be the Son of Man (14:14; Matt. 26:64; 24:27, 30, 37, 39, 44).

2. At His second appearing Christ will be the morning star to His overcomers who watch for His coming (Rev. 22:16; 2:28).

3. Matthew 25:1 indicates that in His coming back Christ will be the Bridegroom, the most pleasant and attractive person in the universe, coming for His bride (Rev. 19:7-9a).

4. At the end of the age of grace, Christ in His coming back will be the Savior to Israel (Rom. 11:26; Zech. 12:10).

5. In Acts 17:31 Paul indicates that Christ in His coming back will be a Judge to the Gentiles.

6. According to Revelation 10:1-7 Christ will come as another Angel to take possession of the earth.

Day 2

B. The revelation of the work of Christ at His coming back:

1. The first aspect of Christ's work at His coming back will be to reap the firstfruits (14:1-5).

2. Toward the end of the tribulation, Christ will catch up the majority of the saints in the clouds (1 Thes. 4:16-17); this will be the reaping of the harvest (Rev. 14:14-16).

3. Christ will set up His judgment seat to judge all the believers, assigning them either a

reward or some kind of punishment (22:12; 2 Cor. 5:10; 1 Cor. 4:5; Rom. 14:10b).

  4. In His work at His coming back, Christ will marry the overcoming saints (Rev. 19:7-9a).

  5. After Christ marries the overcomers, He will slay Antichrist (2 Thes. 2:8; Rev. 19:19-20).

  6. At His coming back Christ will gather and save all the tribes of Israel (1:7; Rom. 11:26; Matt. 24:30-31; Zech. 12:10-14).

  7. In His work at His coming back, Christ will judge the Gentiles, the living peoples (Acts 17:31; Matt. 25:31-46).

Day 3

C. The coming back of Christ has a secret aspect and an open aspect (Rev. 3:3; 16:15; 1:7; 18:1):

  1. In the secret aspect of His coming back, Christ will come as a thief to those who love Him and will take them away as His treasures (3:3; 16:15; Matt. 24:43):

    a. The time of Christ's secret coming is unknown (Rev. 3:3; Matt. 24:36, 42; 25:13).

    b. The place of the secret aspect of Christ's coming will be in the cloud to the air (Rev. 10:1; 1 Thes. 4:17).

    c. Christ's secret coming will be a reward to the watching believers (Rev. 2:28; Matt. 24:42, 44).

  2. In the open aspect of His coming back, Christ will come with power and great glory to be seen by all the tribes of the land (Rev. 1:7):

    a. The time of this open aspect will be at the last trumpet, at the end of the great tribulation (18:1; Matt. 24:15, 21, 27; 1 Thes. 4:16; 1 Cor. 15:52; 2 Thes. 2:1-4, 8).

    b. The place of the open aspect of Christ's coming back will be on the cloud to the earth (Rev. 1:7; 14:14; Matt. 24:30; Zech. 14:4; Acts 1:11-12).

c. When Christ comes openly, He will come with the overcoming saints to fight against Antichrist and his army at Armageddon (Rev. 19:11-21; 17:13-14; 16:12-16; Zech. 14:3, 5; 2 Thes. 2:8).

Day 4 II. **The coming back of Christ is related to the prophecy of the four "sevens" (Dan. 9:24-27; Rev. 5:1; 8:2; 16:1):**

A. The first "seven" is the prophecy concerning the last seven years of the present age—the last of the seventy weeks (Dan. 9:24-27).

B. The second "seven" is the prophecy concerning the seven seals (Rev. 5:1-7; 6:1-17; 8:1-2).

C. The third "seven" is the prophecy concerning the seven trumpets (8:1—9:21; 10:7; 11:15-18).

D. The fourth "seven" is the prophecy concerning the seven bowls (15:7; 16:1-12, 17-21).

E. Nearly all the crucial matters of the final seven years of this present age will be crowded into the last three and a half years, the time of the great tribulation (Matt. 24:21, 29; Dan. 12:1; Rev. 11:15).

Day 5 & Day 6 III. **As believers in Christ, we need to have a proper attitude toward the coming back of Christ (2 Tim. 4:8; Rev. 22:20):**

A. We should love the Lord's appearing (2 Tim. 4:8).

B. We should eagerly await His return and call for His return (Phil. 3:20; 1 Thes. 1:10; Rev. 22:20).

C. We should give heed to the prophetic word as to a lamp shining in a dark place (2 Pet. 1:19).

D. We should be watchful and be ready (Matt. 24:42-44; 25:13).

E. We need to take heed to ourselves lest our hearts be weighed down with debauchery and drunkenness and the anxieties of life (Luke 21:34-35).

F. We need to be watchful at every time, beseeching that we may prevail to escape all the things

which are about to happen and to stand before
the Son of Man (Luke 21:36).

G. We should be prudent virgins and faithful and
prudent slaves (Matt. 25:4, 10; 24:45-51;
25:19-30).

H. We need to keep the word of the Lord's endurance (Rev. 3:10).

Morning Nourishment

Rev. **And he who overcomes and he who keeps My**
2:26 **works until the end, to him I will give authority**
    over the nations.
  28 **And to him I will give the morning star.**
22:16 **I Jesus have sent My angel to testify to you**
    these things for the churches. I am the Root and
    the Offspring of David, the bright morning star.
19:7 **Let us rejoice and exult, and let us give the**
    glory to Him, for the marriage of the Lamb has
    come, and His wife has made herself ready.

Christ's secret coming will be a reward to the watching believers (Rev. 2:28; Matt. 24:42, 44). Revelation 2:28 says that Christ will appear as the morning star, and Malachi 4:2 reveals that He will appear as the sun. There is a great difference between the appearing of the morning star and the appearing of the sun. If you would see the morning star, you must rise up very early in the morning. If you sleep late, you will miss it. However, no matter how late you sleep, you will not miss the sunshine. Do you expect to meet Christ as the morning star or as the sun? The appearing of the morning star is secret, but the appearing of the sun is open. The Lord promised us that if we are watchful and wait for His coming, He will appear to us as the morning star. This is a promise of a reward. But if we are sloppy, we shall surely miss the morning star. (*Life-study of Revelation*, p. 56)

Today's Reading

Christ as the Root and Offspring of David is related to Israel and the kingdom, whereas His being the bright morning star is related to the church and the rapture. The morning star appears before the darkest hour, prior to dawn. The great tribulation will be this darkest hour, after which the day of the kingdom will dawn. In the kingdom the Lord will appear publicly to His people as the sun, but before the great tribulation He will appear privately to His overcomers as the morning star.

Matthew 25:1 indicates that in His coming back Christ will also be the Bridegroom: "At that time the kingdom of the heavens will be likened to ten virgins, who took their lamps and went forth to meet the bridegroom." We are the virgins going and Christ is the Bridegroom coming.

In the Bible we have a universal couple—the Bridegroom and the bride. The bride is the aggregate of regenerated persons, and the Bridegroom is Christ with whom all regenerated persons should be one.

The four Gospels reveal that Christ has come as the Bridegroom (Matt. 9:15; Mark 2:19; Luke 5:34; John 3:29). He has come for His bride, and the bride is His increase (John 3:30). In His coming He will come as the Bridegroom for His bride.

As the Bridegroom the Lord Jesus is the most pleasant and attractive person in the whole universe. He is not only God, the Lord, the Master, and the Savior, but He is also the Bridegroom, the most pleasant person. In His coming back He will be such a Bridegroom.

In Revelation 19:7 Christ is unveiled as having a wedding....The reign of God, the kingdom, is related to the marriage of Christ, and the marriage of Christ is the issue of the completion of God's New Testament economy. God's economy in the New Testament is to obtain for Christ a bride, the church, through His redemption and divine life. By the continual working of the Holy Spirit through all the centuries, this goal will be attained at the end of this age. Then the bride with the overcoming believers will be ready. Hence, in His coming back Christ will be the Bridegroom coming for His bride. According to Revelation 19, He will enjoy a wedding feast. (*Life-study of the New Testament, Conclusion Messages,* pp. 351-352)

Further Reading: Life-study of Revelation, msg. 5; Life-study of the New Testament, Conclusion Messages, msg. 32; The Apostles' Teaching, ch. 10

Enlightenment and inspiration: _____

_____

Morning Nourishment

Rev. And it was given to her that she should be
19:8-9 clothed in fine linen, bright *and* clean; for the
fine linen is the righteousnesses of the saints.
And he said to me, Write, Blessed are they who
are called to the marriage dinner of the Lamb.
And he said to me, These are the true words of
God.

14:15 And another angel came out of the temple, crying with a loud voice to Him who sat on the
cloud, Send forth Your sickle and reap, for the
hour to reap has come because the harvest of
the earth is ripe.

The man-child and the firstfruits, the overcomers, will
be raptured to the third heavens before the last three and
a half years of the great tribulation. The man-child will be
raptured to the throne of God in the heavens, and the
firstfruits will be raptured to Mount Zion in the heavens.
But the majority of the saints will be raptured into the
clouds in the air. They will be raptured after Christ's
parousia travels from the third heavens to the air. While
Christ is lingering in the air, He will rapture all of His
believers. First Thessalonians 4:17 says that the majority
of the believers will be "caught up...in the clouds to meet
the Lord in the air." As believers in Christ, we should all
expect to be raptured, but do we expect to be raptured to
the throne or to the air? The throne is higher than the air.
The throne of God is the peak. To climb a mountain to reach
its peak is not so easy. If we want to be raptured to the
throne, we must overcome. (*The Apostles' Teaching*,
pp. 121-122)

Today's Reading

The words *His wife* in Revelation 19:7 refer to the
church (Eph. 5:24-25, 31-32), the bride of Christ (John

3:29). However, according to Revelation 19:8 and 9, the wife, the bride of Christ, here consists only of the overcoming believers during the millennium, whereas the bride, the wife, in Revelation 21:2 is composed of all the saved saints after the millennium for eternity. The readiness of the bride depends on the maturity in life of the overcomers. Furthermore, the overcomers are not separate individuals but a corporate bride. For this, building is needed. The overcomers are not only mature in life but also built together as the bride.

Righteousnesses [in Revelation 19:8] does not refer to the righteousness we receive for our salvation. The righteousness we receive for salvation is objective so that we may meet the requirement of the righteous God. The righteousnesses of the overcoming saints are subjective so that they may meet the requirements of the overcoming Christ. The fine linen with which the overcomers are clothed is equal to the marriage garment in Matthew 22:11 and 12.

The marriage dinner of the Lamb is the marriage feast in Matthew 22:2. It will be a reward to the overcoming believers. Only the overcomers, not all the saved ones, will be invited to it. The foolish virgins in Matthew 25:8-13 will miss it. However, after being dealt with by the Lord in the kingdom age, they will participate in the New Jerusalem for eternity. Hence, to be invited to the marriage feast of Christ, which will usher the overcoming believers into the enjoyment of the millennium, is to be blessed. The overcoming believers invited to the marriage dinner of the Lamb will also be the bride of the Lamb. Therefore, at His coming back Christ will marry the overcoming saints. (*Life-study of the New Testament, Conclusion Messages*, p. 842)

Further Reading: The Apostles' Teaching, ch. 10; *Life-study of the New Testament, Conclusion Messages*, msg. 78

Enlightenment and inspiration: _____
_____
_____
_____

Morning Nourishment

Rev. ...If therefore you will not watch, I will come as
3:3 a thief, and you shall by no means know at what
hour I will come upon you.
16:15 Behold, I come as a thief. Blessed is he who
watches and keeps his garments that he may not
walk naked and they see his shame.
22:12 Behold, I come quickly, and My reward is with
Me to render to each one as his work is.

Revelation 3:3 and 16:15 both tell us that Christ will come as a thief and that we should be watchful. No thief comes openly or announces his coming....When the Lord comes as a thief, He will come to steal the precious things. In Matthew 24:40 and 41, the Lord spoke of His secret coming, saying, "At that time two men will be in the field; one is taken and one is left. Two women will be grinding at the mill; one is taken and one is left." The Lord Jesus was very wise, using two brothers in the field and two sisters grinding at the mill as illustrations. Apparently the two brothers are the same and the two sisters are the same. But suddenly one of the brothers and one of the sisters are taken. After giving this illustration, the Lord said, "Watch therefore, for you do not know on what day your Lord comes. But know this, that if the householder had known in which watch the thief was coming, he would have watched and would not have allowed his house to be broken into. For this reason you also be ready, because at an hour when you do not expect it, the Son of Man is coming" (vv. 42-44). As we are working, having no consciousness that Christ is coming, some of us will be raptured. Since He is coming as a thief, we must be watchful. (*Life-study of Revelation*, p. 53)

Today's Reading

In the secret aspect of His coming again, Christ will come as a thief. But in the open aspect, He will come with power and great glory to be seen by all the tribes of the land (Rev. 1:7; Matt.

24:27, 30)....While the day and hour of Christ's coming in its secret aspect are unknown (Matt. 24:36), the time of His coming in the second aspect is clearly revealed. It is at the last trumpet (the seventh trumpet), at the end of the great tribulation (Rev. 18:1; Matt. 24:15, 21, 27; 1 Thes. 4:16; 1 Cor. 15:52; 2 Thes. 2:1-4, 8).

The place of the open aspect of the Lord's coming back is clearly revealed—on the cloud to the earth (Rev. 1:7; 14:14; Matt. 24:30; Zech. 14:4; Acts 1:11-12). According to Acts 1:11 and 12, the Lord shall come in the same way as He went up into heaven. Since He ascended from the Mount of Olives, this means that He will come back to the Mount of Olives....The Lord will descend to the very spot from which He ascended. However, we are not waiting to see Him on the Mount of Olives. We want to meet Him at the throne in the third heaven and then come back with Him to the Mount of Olives.

When the Lord Jesus comes openly, He will come with the overcoming saints to fight against the Antichrist and his army at Armageddon (Rev. 19:11-21; 17:13-14; 16:12-16; Zech. 14:3, 5; 2 Thes. 2:8). This will be to tread the winepress of the wrath of God (Rev. 19:15; 14:18-20). At Armageddon, all the worldly armies will be gathered together....In the eyes of God, the earthly armies are likened to grapes, and Armageddon will be the great winepress....Then the Lord will descend to tread this winepress of God, and a great river of blood will flow out of it. What a huge number of evil people will be killed there at that time! This will occur at the time of the Lord's open coming to the earth. The purpose of the Lord's open coming will be to exterminate all the worldly forces. After this, war will cease from the earth.

In 22:12 and 20 the Lord Jesus gives us a warning, saying, "Behold, I come quickly." Our loving response should be, "Amen. Come, Lord Jesus" (22:20; 2 Tim. 4:8). Our concern in these messages is not with mere teaching and doctrine concerning the so-called second advent. We are studying the heart's desire of the Lord, which is to gain a group of overcomers who are watching and waiting for His coming back. (*Life-study of Revelation,* pp. 57-61)

Further Reading: Life-study of Revelation, msg. 5

Enlightenment and inspiration: _____
_____

Morning Nourishment

Rev. And I saw on the right hand of Him who sits upon
5:1 the throne a scroll written within and on the
back, sealed up with seven seals.

Matt. So also you, when you see all these things, know
24:33 that it is near, at the doors.

2 Pet. And we have the prophetic word *made* more
1:19 firm, to which you do well to give heed as to a
lamp shining in a dark place, until the day dawns
and the morning star rises in your hearts.

Because of the world situation today, I believe that our present study of the prophecy of the four "sevens" in the Bible is timely. Romans 9:27-28 says that the Lord will cut His word short in order to have a quick fulfillment of His prophecy concerning the nation of Israel. The present situation in the Middle East is the Lord cutting His word short so that the prophecies concerning Israel can be fulfilled quickly....The nation of Israel as the fig tree has become tender and put forth its leaves. Now the summer is near (Matt. 24:32). We are not teaching the biblical prophecies to satisfy people's curiosity. We desire to be enlightened by the Word, especially the prophetic word in the Bible. We need to give heed to this prophetic word as to a lamp shining in a dark place (2 Pet. 1:19). Then we will know where we are. The prophetic word will guide us to pass through the dark night until the day of the Lord's appearing dawns and the morning star rises in our hearts. (*The Prophecy of the Four "Sevens" in the Bible*, pp. 54-55)

Today's Reading

In Matthew 24:36 the Lord said, "Concerning that day and hour, no one knows, not even the angels of the heavens nor the Son, but the Father only." According to the context of this word, Matthew 24:32-44, *that day and hour* refers to the day and hour of the rapture of the overcomers into the secret section of His parousia (coming) in the third heavens. That day and hour no one knows but the Father only who keeps that day and hour in Himself as secrecy.

However, the year of the appearing of the public section of His parousia (coming) to the earth can be figured out according to the last week (seven years) of the seventy weeks revealed in Daniel 9:24-27. According to Daniel's prophecy, at the coming of the last week, Antichrist will make a firm covenant with Israel for seven years, and at the midst of the seven years, he will break that covenant and persecute the people of Israel and the remaining believers (Dan. 9:27). When the believers see the coming Antichrist making a covenant with the Jews for seven years, we can figure out, by the prophecies in Matthew 24:15-44; 1 Corinthians 15:51-52; 1 Thessalonians 4:15-17; 2 Thessalonians 2:1-8; and Revelation 6—16, the year of the rapture of the overcomers which should probably be in the first half of the fourth year of the last week, and the year of the rapture of the majority of the saints and of the two witnesses which will be the last year of the last week. We can even figure out the day of the rapture of the majority of the saints and the two witnesses which will be the last day of the last week.

The Lord in Matthew 24:32-33 gives us some signs that we may know the period of His parousia which will be in the last part of the last week. The Lord says, "Learn the parable from the fig tree: As soon as its branch has become tender and puts forth its leaves." The fig tree here symbolizes the nation of Israel which was condemned by the Lord to be dried up in Matthew 21:19, and the branch becoming tender and putting forth its leaves signifies the restoration of the nation of Israel which has taken place already. By this kind of sign, we have to realize that we are now in a time which is very close to the last week of the present age. Hence, we have to be more on the alert to get ourselves prepared for the Lord's parousia (coming). (*The Apostles' Teaching*, pp. 114-115)

Further Reading: The Prophecy of the Four "Sevens" in the Bible, ch. 3; The Apostles' Teaching, ch. 9; Life-study of Daniel, msg. 14

Enlightenment and inspiration: _____

Morning Nourishment

Rev. Because you have kept the word of My endur-
3:10 ance, I also will keep you out of the hour of trial,
which is about to come on the whole inhabited
earth, to try them who dwell on the earth.

22:20 He who testifies these things says, Yes, I come
quickly. Amen. Come, Lord Jesus!

2 Tim. Henceforth there is laid up for me the crown of
4:8 righteousness, with which the Lord, the righteous
Judge, will recompense me in that day, and not only
me but also all those who have loved His appearing.

We also need to keep the word of Christ's endurance that we
may be kept by Him out of the hour of trial which will come on
the whole inhabited earth, to try those who dwell on the earth
(Rev. 3:10). Today the word we keep is the word of endurance.
As long as we keep the word of God, we will suffer. People will
persecute us. Even our parents and relatives may despise us.
We need to keep the Lord's word of endurance so that we may
be kept out of the time of the great tribulation as a trial which
will come on the whole inhabited earth to try those who dwell
on the earth. We have to be watchful and ready to learn the
spiritual lessons. To become matured is not an overnight matter.
Therefore, we have to prepare ourselves for His coming by
loving Him so that we can grow in Him and be matured for His
appearing. (*The Prophecy of the Four "Sevens" in the Bible*, p. 24)

We may express our desire for the Lord's return in the way
of a prayer to Him, calling, "Come, Lord Jesus!" (Rev. 22:20). We
should always call for His coming. This becomes our response
to His return. (*The Vision of the Divine Dispensing and Guidelines for the Practice of the New Way*, p. 42)

Today's Reading

Since we know that the Lord's second coming is so precious,
we should love the Lord's appearing (2 Tim. 4:8). The Bible
concludes with "Come, Lord Jesus!" (Rev. 22:20). From the

record in the New Testament, it is not difficult to discover that in their hearts the apostles firmly believed that the Lord would come quickly, and they also lived a life in preparation for the Lord's second coming....Do not think that since we are clear concerning the signs of the Lord's coming, we can be slothful and can first love the world and then pursue the Lord when the last week comes. There is no such convenience. We should believe that the Lord is to be feared. In Luke 12 the Lord gave a parable concerning a rich man who endeavored to lay up wealth for himself so that his soul might enjoy itself and be merry. But God said to him, "Foolish one, this night they are requiring your soul from you" (vv. 16-20). Every "today" that we have is truly the Lord's grace. Therefore, as long as we have today, as long as we still have breath, we should love the Lord and His appearing, await the Lord's coming (Phil. 3:20), and always take His coming as an encouragement.

In 2 Timothy 4:1 Paul said to Timothy, "I solemnly charge you before God and Christ Jesus, who is to judge the living and the dead, and by His appearing and His kingdom." This is an exhortation from Paul immediately before his martyrdom. He said that he had fought the good fight, he had finished the course, and he had kept the faith, and that at the judgment seat he would be awarded the crown of righteousness, which would be awarded to all those who have loved His appearing (2 Tim. 4:6-8). He reminded Timothy, and also us, by the Lord's judgment and kingdom that we should have a living that loves the Lord's appearing. This will cause us not to be discouraged, not to backslide, not to become weak, but to remain faithful to the end. (*The Up-to-date Presentation of the God-ordained Way and the Signs concerning the Coming of Christ*, pp. 67-69)

Further Reading: The Prophecy of the Four "Sevens" in the Bible, ch. 1; *The Vision of the Divine Dispensing and Guidelines for the Practice of the New Way,* ch. 4; *The Up-to-date Presentation of the God-ordained Way and the Signs concerning the Coming of Christ,* ch. 7; *The Practical Expression of the Church,* ch. 22

Enlightenment and inspiration: _____

_____

_____

Morning Nourishment

Luke But take heed to yourselves lest perhaps your
21:34 hearts be weighed down with debauchery and
drunkenness and the anxieties of life, and that
day come upon you suddenly as a snare.

35 For it will come in upon all those dwelling on the
face of all the earth.

Phil. For our commonwealth exists in the heavens,
3:20 from which also we eagerly await a Savior, the
Lord Jesus Christ.

1 Thes. For God did not appoint us to wrath but to the
5:9-10 obtaining of salvation through our Lord Jesus
Christ, who died for us in order that whether we
watch or sleep, we may live together with Him.

We need to be on guard that our hearts would not be weighed down with debauchery, drunkenness, and anxieties of life. Debauchery is indulgence in drinking and feasting. If our heart is full of anxieties, then it has no room for God, for Christ. We may even come to a meeting, but our heart is not in that meeting because it is preoccupied with worldly things. We need to guard our hearts because we do not want the day of the great tribulation to come upon us unexpectedly as a snare. This day will be like the flood which came unexpectedly to the people at Noah's time. We need to watch and pray that we may prevail to escape all these things and stand before the Son of Man. This corresponds with Revelation 14:1, which indicates that the raptured overcomers will stand before the Savior on Mount Zion in the heavens before the great tribulation (cf. Rev. 12:5-6, 14). (*The Prophecy of the Four "Sevens" in the Bible*, pp. 23-24)

Today's Reading

The world is over, and the Lord is coming back. We are not children of darkness, but children of light; so everything is clear to us. The people of the world are dreaming about peace and safety, but it will never come. The Lord is coming back; so let us be wise and sober. Let the people of the world be foolish. While they are crying for peace and safety, the Lord will return.

Brothers and sisters, how can we be prepared for the Lord's coming? First Thessalonians 5:9-10...corresponds with all the ministry in the past years. We must learn to live with Him, to be one with Him by always turning to our spirit. To live with Christ means to be one with Him. Whatever you say, you must say together with Him. Wherever you go, you must go together with Him. We must simply be one with Him. In our home, we must be one with Him. In school, we must be one with Him. In our business, we must be one with Him. We must live with Christ in our spirit. This is the proper way for us to be prepared.

If we would take this one step to live with Christ, we will immediately be turned. We will be turned to the heavenly way from the world. Jesus is near. Jerusalem has been returned, and the whole world is talking about peace and safety. This is the strongest sign that this is the end of this age. The coming of the Lord Jesus is imminent. Therefore, we must be transformed and built up in a local expression of His Body that we may be prepared as His bride for His return. (*The Practical Expression of the Church*, pp. 187-188)

Since we love the Lord's appearing, we should earnestly wait for His coming (Phil. 3:20; 1 Thes. 1:10). Hence, our future is with Him. Our living should indicate that we have no other hope on this earth. Our hope is in the coming Lord. He is our eternal destiny. In 1 Corinthians 7 Paul says, "But this I say, brothers, the time is shortened. Henceforth...those who buy [should be] as though they did not possess, and those who use the world as though they did not abuse it; for the fashion of this world is passing away" (vv. 29-31). Christ is our real hope. (*The Vision of the Divine Dispensing and Guidelines for the Practice of the New Way*, p. 42)

Further Reading: The Prophecy of the Four "Sevens" in the Bible, ch. 1; The Practical Expression of the Church, ch. 22; The Vision of the Divine Dispensing and Guidelines for the Practice of the New Way, ch. 4

Enlightenment and inspiration: _____

Hymns, #960

1 My King will soon come back again,
    The sky be filled with Him;
  The universe to be redeemed
    Will see His light therein.
  The Lord will soon fulfill His plan,
    His footsteps now I hear;
  His glorious frame I faintly see
    Beginning to appear.

2 I'm longing for His presence blest
    And dare not slothful be
  While waiting for my Lord's return,
    His own dear self to see.
  My only hope—that He may come
    And change my faith to sight;
  There is no other joy on earth
    Which gives my heart delight.

3 My heart is always with Himself,
    My eyes are heavenward,
  My lips would utter nothing else
    Than meeting with my Lord.
  The coming of the Lord draws nigh,
    His coming is for me;
  His promise ever standeth firm
    And soon fulfilled I'll see.

4 My Savior, all Thy holy words
    Can never doubted be;
  With them encouraged day by day,
    I'm faithful unto Thee.
  Oh, may Thy glory soon appear,
    The foe be overthrown;
  Thy promises be realized,
    And we brought to Thy throne.

5 Thy saving arm a refuge is,
    My Savior God, to me;
  Thou as the Father keepeth them
    Who put their trust in Thee.
  The sheep and shepherd are of one,
    The head and body same;
  None e'er can pluck from out Thy hand
    The child who trusts Thy Name.

6   A thousand hands won't hinder me,
     Nor will ten thousand eyes;
   The thorns upon the road but help
     Me onward to the prize.
   Arise, my spirit and my heart,
     And let the world go by;
   The Lord of life will take me soon
     To be with Him on high.

7   Thou healing sun! Thou hope of man!
     I really love Thy ray.
   Oh, righteous Lord! oh, glorious King!
     I bow to Thee and pray:
   Oh, may Thou soon ascend Thy throne
     And quickly show Thy face;
   Thy heav'nly kingdom may Thou found
     And grant all men Thy grace.

8   The truth should triumph and be king,
     And freedom should be queen;
   But falsehood, which has rampant run,
     Head of the world be seen.
   We ask Thee, Truth, to quickly come
     And bring Thy light from heav'n;
   The foe be crushed and all Thy sons
     Into Thy bosom giv'n.

Composition for prophecy with main point and sub-points: _____

_____
_____
_____
_____
_____
_____
_____
_____
_____
_____
_____
_____
_____
_____

The Intrinsic Significance and
Subjective Experience
of the Golden Lampstand

Scripture Reading: Exo. 25:31-40; Zech. 4:1-14; Rev. 1:10-12, 20

Day 1   **I. We need a spirit of wisdom and revelation to
understand the significance of the golden
lampstand, which was designed by God Himself and portrays the goal of His eternal economy (Eph. 1:17; Zech. 4:1-5; Rev. 1:2, 9-12):**

   A. The golden lampstand signifies the Triune God:

     1. The pure gold substance signifies God the
Father in His divine nature (Exo. 25:31).

     2. The stand signifies God the Son as the em-
bodiment of God the Father (2 Cor. 4:4b; Col.
1:15; 2:9).

     3. The lamps signify God the Spirit as the seven
Spirits of God for the expression of the Father in the Son (Exo. 25:37; Rev. 4:5).

   B. The golden lampstands signify the local
churches as the reproduction of Christ and the
reprint of the Spirit:

     1. The lampstand in Exodus 25 signifies Christ
as the embodiment of God (vv. 31-40).

     2. The lampstand in Zechariah 4 signifies the
sevenfold intensified, life-giving Spirit as the
reality of Christ (vv. 2, 6, 10; Rev. 5:6).

     3. The lampstands in Revelation 1 are the re-
print, the reproduction, of this Spirit-Christ
(vv. 11-12, 20).

Day 2   **II. We need to subjectively experience the detailed aspects of the golden lampstand so that
we can become the reproduction of the lampstand, the expression of the Triune God:**

   A. The lampstand is of pure gold, signifying the
eternal, incorruptible, divine nature of God
(Exo. 25:31):

1. We need to pay the price to gain more gold, more of God in His divine nature (2 Pet. 1:4; Rev. 3:18; Zech. 4:12-14; Matt. 25:8-9).

2. Mixture in our Christian life brings in darkness, but when our Christian life is purified through the divine nature, we have light (cf. Deut. 22:9).

B. The lampstand is of beaten work, signifying sufferings (Exo. 25:31):

1. To be beaten is to participate in Christ's sufferings for the producing and building up of the Body of Christ (1 Pet. 4:1; Phil. 3:10; Col. 1:24; Acts 16:6-7).

2. We must be beaten together with others into one entity, blended together through the cross and by the Spirit (1 Cor. 12:24), to shine forth the light of God for His corporate testimony.

C. The lampstand being without measurement signifies that the divinity of Christ and the light He shines are immeasurable (John 3:34; cf. 7:18; 1 Cor. 2:13).

D. The lampstand's base for stability and its shaft for strength signify that the Lord Jesus was always stable and strong (Matt. 8:24; cf. 2 Cor. 1:18; Rev. 1:9).

Day 3   E. The lampstand's having cups shaped like almond blossoms with calyxes and blossoming buds signifies that the Triune God is a living, golden tree, growing, budding, and blossoming in resurrection (Exo. 25:31):

1. The cups shaped like almond blossoms signify the resurrection life blossoming (Num. 17:8; Jer. 1:11-12):

a. The blossoming of resurrection life is the shining light, the expression of the life of God, the fruit of the Spirit and the fruit of the light (John 1:4; Gal. 5:22; Eph. 5:9).

b. If we would shine forth the light of life, we must be in resurrection, not in our natural life (Phil. 3:10; S. S. 2:8-9, 14; cf. Psa. 73:16-17).

c. Christ as the resurrection life is growing, branching, budding, and blossoming in us, by us, and with us to shine the light (Col. 2:19).

d. How much light there can be in the church depends on the extent to which Christ has a way to grow in us and through us.

2. As those who believe in Christ, we are a part of this wonderful golden tree in resurrection and with the divine nature, life, the Spirit, and the shining light.

Day 4   F. The pure golden snuffers and snuff dishes for trimming the charred wicks signify the dealing with the old and charred natural life by the divine nature so that the shining of the resurrection life may be bright and pure (Exo. 25:38).

G. The lampstand with all its utensils was one talent of pure gold (one hundred pounds), signifying that Christ as the divine lampstand shining the divine light in resurrection is perfectly and completely weighty (John 7:45-46; 18:37-38; cf. 1 Tim. 2:2; Titus 2:7).

Day 5   H. The seven lamps of the lampstand are the seven Spirits of God as the seven eyes of Jehovah (Zech. 4:10), the seven eyes of the redeeming Lamb (Rev. 5:6), and the seven eyes of the building stone (Zech. 3:9) for the full expression of the Triune God:

1. "No Spirit, no church. More Spirit, more church" (Zech. 4:6).

2. The seven eyes of the Lamb infuse us with Christ as the judicial Redeemer, and the

seven eyes of the stone infuse us with Christ as the organic Savior for God's economical move on earth through His redemption and by His organic salvation for the goal of His building (John 1:29; Acts 4:11-12; Rom. 5:10; 1 Cor. 3:12).

Day 6

3. Within us we have two lamps—the sevenfold intensified Spirit of God within our spirit (Prov. 20:27; Rev. 4:5; 1 Cor. 6:17):

   a. In order for us to be transformed, we must fully open to the Lord in prayer to allow the lamp of the Lord with the seven lamps of fire to search all the chambers of our soul, shining on and enlightening our inward parts to supply them with life (1 Cor. 2:11a; Eph. 6:18).

   b. The one who experiences the greatest transformation is the one who is fully open to the Lord.

4. The more we experience the detailed aspects of the Triune God depicted in the lampstand, the more we will see the reproduction of the lampstand, which will pave the way for the Lord's coming back to possess the whole earth.

Morning Nourishment

Exo. **And you shall make a lampstand of pure gold.**
25:31 **The lampstand *with* its base and its shaft shall be made of beaten work; its cups, its calyxes, and its blossom buds shall be of *one piece with* it.**
Rev. **The mystery of...the seven golden lampstands:...**
1:20 **The seven lampstands are the seven churches.**

We all have to see that the church is an exact reproduction of Christ. Christ was the unique lampstand, and all the churches are the lampstands in the same nature, essence, model, shape, and function. According to the lampstand in Exodus we can say that the church is the reproduction of Christ, and according to the lampstand in Zechariah the church is the reprint of the Spirit. The ultimate definition of the church is that the church is the reproduction of Christ and the reprint of the Spirit.

When we say that we are the church, we have to realize that the church is the reproduction of Christ and the reprint of the Spirit. When we say that we are the church, we must realize that we have to be fully in the Spirit. Even if we are only partially in the flesh, we become a poor reproduction, a poor reprint. When we brothers and sisters come together, if we all are in the Spirit, we are the church. If we are outside of the Spirit, we are not the church. Whether or not we are actually the church depends upon whether or not we are in the Spirit. (*The Church—the Reprint of the Spirit,* pp. 11-12)

Today's Reading

Among all the furniture in the tabernacle, the lampstand was unique. Nearly every piece of furniture in the tabernacle had wood, except for the laver, which was made of brass. The altar, the showbread table, the incense altar, and the ark were all made of acacia wood overlaid with brass or gold. But the lampstand had no wood. It was altogether one piece of pure gold. Although the laver had no wood, it also had no gold since it was made of brass. The lampstand was a pure piece of gold, and the church is the reprint of the lampstand. Thus, the wood has to be eliminated. The wood has to be reduced. When the church is seen as the testimony of Jesus in Revelation, all the churches are pure golden lampstands because every local church is a reproduction of Christ, and Christ today is the life-giving Spirit.

If our eyes are opened by the Lord, and we see this vision concerning the church, this vision will be better than a thousand messages concerning the church. If you have really seen this vision, you will not exercise your mind to argue with the brothers in your locality. When the sisters are exercising their emotions to do something, this vision will terminate them. Even at the dining table this vision will be shining to govern us. We need a governing vision that terminates, kills, and annuls everything of our natural man. When a brother is about to exchange words with his wife, this vision will terminate him. When you are about to vindicate yourself, the Lord may say, "What's that?—natural!" If this vision is shining so brightly within us, the Lord will have a way to speak to us in our daily life to terminate our natural man. He will be able to say: "What's that?—natural love! What's that?—natural thinking! What's that?—your natural man! What's that?—natural, natural, natural!" Everything that is natural has to go. Otherwise, we actually are not in the church. Although you were put into the church nineteen and a half centuries ago, actually today you may not be in the church. Where are you? You may be in the natural life. We have to rise up to testify that the church is the reprint of the Spirit. We need to testify, "From now on, my natural being has no share in the church, no part in the church, because I have seen that the church is the reprint of the Spirit!" The church as the lampstand is pure and without mixture. The church is the embodiment of Christ and the reprint of the Spirit. (*The Church—the Reprint of the Spirit*, pp. 23-24)

Further Reading: The Church—the Reprint of the Spirit, chs. 1, 3; *Life Messages,* vol. 2, ch. 68; *Elders' Training, Book 7: One Accord for the Lord's Move,* ch. 3

Enlightenment and inspiration: _____

Morning Nourishment

Exo. **And you shall make a lampstand of pure gold.**
25:31 **The lampstand *with* its base and its shaft shall be made of beaten work; its cups, its calyxes, and its blossom buds shall be of *one piece with* it.**
   39 **It shall be made of a talent of pure gold....**
John **God is Spirit, and those who worship Him must**
4:24 **worship in spirit and truthfulness.**

We all need to experience the golden element of the lampstand. If we only have an ounce of gold, how could we form a lampstand? This would be impossible. We might be able to make a ring, but certainly not a lampstand. In order to have a lampstand, there must be a talent of gold (Exo. 25:39). (A talent equals approximately one hundred pounds, or sixteen hundred ounces.) We need more gold, more of God. If we would have the church as the lampstand, we must have something substantial—the gold, which is the substance, the essence, the element, of God Himself....How we need God as the golden element! (*Life-study of Revelation,* pp. 363-364)

Today's Reading

Beaten work signifies sufferings. To be beaten is to suffer. When Christ, the embodiment of God, was on earth, He experienced much suffering, much beating.

With the ark, the gold was beaten to express the glory of God. The two cherubim were made of gold which had been beaten. These cherubim of glory signify that the glory of God comes out of the beating, that the glory of God expressed in Christ comes out of His sufferings.

With the lampstand, the gold was beaten to shine forth the light of God. This light equals the glory of God. This means that the light on the lampstand equals the glory above the ark. Both came out of gold which had been beaten. This indicates that through His sufferings Christ expresses God's glory.

If we are short of sufferings, our light may not shine brightly.

Although we should not seek to suffer, we should not despise sufferings, for they are useful. If we never experience any difficulties, any beating of the gold, we shall not be able to shine. For example, if your husband or wife or your children are always good to you, this may hinder your shining. But if you face difficulties in your family life, these difficulties will help you to shine. Children can be compared to little hammers, hammers which beat the gold within their parents and help them to shine. (*Life-study of Exodus*, pp. 1073-1074)

If you would have the stand, you must be beaten together with others. You need to lose your identification. Do not say, "This is my gold. I'm spiritual." For you to be spiritual as an end in itself is meaningless as far as the lampstand is concerned. Your experience and enjoyment of God must be beaten together with that of others. Our gold must be put together, beaten, and built up as one entity, as one unit. Then we not only have the gold, but are also built into a golden lampstand. This is the church.

If those in the church in Anaheim are merely several hundred individual units, we are finished. God does not desire hundreds of individual units of gold. He wants all the gold put together and beaten to form the lampstand. What a need there is for the building! If we have seen the building, we will never be individualistic. Rather, we would realize that whatever we gain or receive of the divine element is for the building of the lampstand. Because God's desire is for the building, we have given message after message saying that we need God in Christ as our very substance that we might be built together. It is good to have a large quantity of gold and thereby to be rich in God. But are you still individualistic, or are you part of a corporate entity? We need the building. (*Life-study of Revelation*, p. 366)

Further Reading: Life-study of Revelation, msg. 31; *Life-study of Exodus,* msgs. 92-94

Enlightenment and inspiration: _____

_____

_____

_____

Morning Nourishment

Exo. **And you shall make a lampstand of pure gold.**
25:31 **The lampstand *with* its base and its shaft shall be made of beaten work; its cups, its calyxes, and its blossom buds shall be of *one piece with* it.**

Phil. **To know Him and the power of His resurrection**
3:10 **and the fellowship of His sufferings, being conformed to His death.**

Col. **...Holding the Head, out from whom all the Body,**
2:19 **being richly supplied and knit together by means of the joints and sinews, grows with the growth of God.**

The cups, the calyxes, the external green leafy parts of the flowers, containing the blossom buds, signify the sustaining and supporting power of the resurrection life. We can comprehend this only through our experience with the Lord. To shine the divine light is to blossom....In order to shine with the divine light, we must have resurrection life to be a cup, a calyx, as a container to sustain and support our shining. If we do not have resurrection life as such a container, our blossom will collapse. This means that the shining of the divine light in us will cease. Without the cups, the calyxes, the flowering buds would fall. In like manner, without the resurrection life, we have nothing to uphold, support, and sustain our shining of the divine light.

When you remain in resurrection, you are blossoming, shining. But when you leave resurrection and return to your natural life, you immediately stop shining. You may have been shining a few minutes ago, but now, having lost the support of resurrection life, you are no longer shining. Whenever the calyx, the support of the blossoming bud, is removed, the flower collapses and falls. Thus, because there is no blossoming, there is no shining. The shining of the divine light is held by the resurrection life. (*Life-study of Exodus*, pp. 1076-1077)

Today's Reading

As a tree, the lampstand has certain outstanding features.

First, it is a golden tree. Gold signifies the nature of God....The golden lampstand is the expression of the Triune God. The Triune God is a living tree, growing, budding, and blossoming.

We have seen that this golden tree has many almond blossoms. In typology almonds signify resurrection life. Aaron's rod budding with almonds signifies resurrection life. Hence, the almonds on the lampstand indicate that it is a tree in resurrection....Resurrection is life which passes through death and can never be held by it. According to the full revelation of the Scriptures, God Himself is this resurrection life.

The lampstand, of course, gives light. However, the first significance of the lampstand is not light, but life. The light is at the top of the lampstand and underneath this shining light are the blossoms. The lampstand is something that grows. The calyx under each pair of branches indicates the growth of life. These branches are produced by the growing of life. Thus, with the lampstand we see the branching out of life which takes place under the shining of the light. Life grows out light and blossoms with light. This means that the light is actually the blossoming of life. When we grow and blossom, the light shines. Our blossoming is our shining. We grow with life, but we blossom out light.

Thus far, we have seen that with the lampstand we have the divine nature, resurrection, life, and light. The seven lamps on the lampstand (v. 37) signify the Spirit. Therefore, with the lampstand there are five crucial matters: the divine nature, resurrection, life, the Spirit, and light. The revelation in the Bible, especially in the New Testament, corresponds to the lampstand in these five matters—the divine nature, resurrection, life, the Spirit, and light.

Now we must see that as those who believe in Christ, we are a part of this wonderful tree. Realizing that I am part of this golden tree causes me to be beside myself with joy. Praise the Lord that we are parts of this tree in resurrection and with the divine nature, life, the Spirit, and the shining light! (*Life-study of Exodus*, pp. 1083-1084)

Further Reading: Life-study of Exodus, msgs. 92-94

Enlightenment and inspiration: _____

Morning Nourishment

Exo. And its tongs and its firepans shall be of pure
25:38 gold.
   39 It shall be made of a talent of pure gold, with
      all these utensils.
Phil. That you may be blameless and guileless, chil-
2:15 dren of God without blemish in the midst of a
      crooked and perverted generation, among
      whom you shine as luminaries in the world.

The wick was the only part of the lampstand that was not made of gold. Thus, the wick signifies not divinity but humanity. Furthermore, the fact that the wick could become charred indicates that the lampstand not only signifies Christ Himself, but also us. Christ's humanity could never produce a charred wick. Only our humanity is capable of becoming burnt and charred. Surely Christ had no need of the tongs to trim Him, to deal with Him. As we read the four Gospels, we realize that it was never necessary for Christ to be snuffed, for there was never a charred wick in His human living. However, we easily become charred and need to be snuffed every day.

Morning watch is an excellent time to experience the Lord's trimming, His snuffing. I can testify that this trimming takes place as I make confession to the Lord and ask Him to forgive me of all my defects, failures, weaknesses, and wrongdoings. If we consider our situation each day, we shall see that there is always some charred wick that needs to be snuffed. Our humanity is very low compared to Christ's humanity. His humanity never produces any snuff, but ours produces snuff every day and requires a daily trimming. Thus, in our experience we need the tongs and the firepans. (*Life-study of Exodus*, pp. 1085-1086)

Today's Reading

[An] aspect of the lampstand related to the humanity of

Christ is the wick. The wick was made of fibers, primarily of cotton. When the lamps on the stand were lighted, the wick burned with the oil. Every morning it was necessary for the priests to trim the lamps, that is, to snuff the charred, burnt wick. The charred portion of the wick is called snuff. The word *snuff* is also a verb meaning to cut off the burnt part of the wick. Exodus 25:38 speaks of the tongs and the firepans. The tongs were used to cut the wick, and the firepans were used to contain the burnt part of the wick. When the priest trimmed the lamps every morning, he cut off the charred wick and also added fresh oil. This was the priests' work in caring for the lampstand.

Perhaps you are wondering who performs this work of trimming, or snuffing. Often Christ Himself will snuff us during times of fellowship with Him in the morning. At other times He may use an elder or one of the saints to do this. Furthermore, the ministers of the Word also snuff the saints and trim them. If you are a Christian who is growing and maturing in the Lord, you will unconsciously snuff others as you have fellowship with them. Some have told me that, during the course of fellowship, they have been snuffed by me. Of course, I had no intention of trimming anyone. This happened unconsciously and unintentionally. For example, one brother told me that something I said in fellowship helped him with respect to a problem he had with his wife. He told me that this cutting, this snuffing, was very helpful to him.

Many Christians today are not shining because they have a long, charred wick. Their charred wick is smoking rather than shining. In some cases, the wick may be more than twelve inches long! In order to shine properly and adequately, we need the snuffing. (*Life-study of Exodus*, pp. 1085-1086)

Further Reading: Life-study of Exodus, msg. 93

Enlightenment and inspiration: _____

_____

_____

_____

Morning Nourishment

Zech. And he answered and spoke to me, saying, This
4:6 is the word of Jehovah to Zerubbabel, saying, Not
by might nor by power, but by My Spirit, says
Jehovah of hosts.

Rev. ...And *there were* seven lamps of fire burning before
4:5 the throne, which are the seven Spirits of God.

5:6 And I saw in the midst of the throne and of the
four living creatures and in the midst of the elders
a Lamb standing as having *just* been slain, having
seven horns and seven eyes, which are the seven
Spirits of God sent forth into all the earth.

[Another] item we need to see is the Spirit for the Body. The
Spirit is for many positive items of the Christian life, but
ultimately the Spirit is for the Body. The Spirit is for regeneration, sanctification, transformation, life, power, and so many
spiritual items, but all of these items are altogether for one
issue—the Body. Regeneration, sanctification, transformation,
life, power, and every positive spiritual blessing are for the Body.
If we miss the Body, we miss everything. If we miss the Body,
we miss the mark and the goal of God's economy.

The Spirit is for the Body, so 1 Corinthians 12:13 says that
in one Spirit we were all baptized into one Body, and Ephesians
4:4 says, "One Body and one Spirit." The one Spirit equals the
one Body, and the one Body equals the one Spirit. Thus, it is
absolutely correct to say that the church is the reprint of the
Spirit. "No Spirit, no church. More Spirit, more church." This is
because the church is the reprint of the Spirit. The Spirit is the
ultimate consummation of the processed Triune God, and the
church is the reprint of the Spirit, the corporate expression of
the processed Triune God. (*The Church—the Reprint of the
Spirit*, pp. 19-20)

Today's Reading

Before I came into the church, I was saved and was loving

the Lord. I did not love the world. Rather, I was a clean, young Christian who sought the Lord, studied the Bible, and prayed every day. However, after I came into the church, I was thoroughly searched, not by any teacher, but by something within.... I experienced the searching and made a thorough confession to the Lord....Many of us have had a similar experience. This was the experience of the enlightening, the searching, the exposing, and the judging of the Lord. I can still recall the judgment I underwent as I came to the meetings. I hated myself, my nature, my old man, and my disposition....He seemed to be saying, "You are so fleshly, so natural, and so much in yourself. You are still too much in the old creation."...This was the work of the flaming lamps in the church. I had never experienced this before.

As a result of this flaming of the seven lamps, the Lord Jesus became so precious, so dear, and so lovable to me. Never before had I had such a deep sense of the Lord's preciousness and loveliness. This was the transfusing and infusing of the Lord Jesus Himself into my being. How dear, precious, and available the Lord was to me! He was a lovely treasure to me. I loved Him more than ever before. I had truly been infused with Him. I can testify that during that time I was in the third heaven and that every sin and weakness was under my feet. I had no need to try to overcome anything.

Following this infusing, there was the impartation of life. The seven lamps became the seven eyes, and the seven eyes became the seven Spirits. The enlightening, searching, exposing, and judging issued in the transfusing of the Lord Jesus into me, and this transfusion resulted in the impartation of life. I received more life, the life which is just Christ Himself. More of Christ was added into my being. He was imparted deeply into my whole being....As a result, I had some transformation, and I loved the church and all the saints meeting with me. This was the building. (*Life-study of Revelation,* pp. 393-394)

Further Reading: The Church—the Reprint of the Spirit, ch. 2; *Life-study of Revelation,* msgs. 8, 33

Enlightenment and inspiration: _____

_____

_____

Morning Nourishment

Prov. The spirit of man is the lamp of Jehovah, search-
20:27 ing all the innermost parts [rooms] of the inner
being.
Rev. ...And *there were* seven lamps of fire burning before
4:5 the throne, which are the seven Spirits of God.
1 Cor. But he who is joined to the Lord is one spirit.
6:17

Who experiences the greatest amount of transformation? It
is the one who is absolutely open to the Lord.

"Lord, I am fully open to You. I want to keep opening to You.
My whole being is open—my heart, my mind, my will, and my
emotions. Keep shining. Search me thoroughly. Enlighten and
enliven me. I will accept it fully." In this way, the light will
penetrate into every area, and life simultaneously will be
supplied to you. The man of clay will be transformed into the
image of Christ. As the gold is thus formed in you, there will be
the seven Spirits shining forth and manifesting God.

Such is the church in reality. The golden lampstand is not
only the Triune God; it also is the church, His manifestation.
That the church may express the Triune God is what He is
working to accomplish on earth.

May we all be open to Him to receive His enlightening and
to let His life supply us. Then we shall be transformed and bear
the image of Christ. As we are enlightened by the lamps within
us, we shall become the golden lampstand in reality in our
locality, manifesting the Triune God. Then He will have His
testimony. (*Life Messages,* pp. 248-249)

Today's Reading

Your spirit is now a lamp indwelt by the Spirit of God, who
is also a lamp. The spirit wants to enlighten every part of your
soul. By responding to the spirit's shining, you will be walking
"according to the spirit" (Rom. 8:4).

Sometimes when God wants to shine in us, we will not open
to Him. This is why, after we have been praying for a while, we

sometimes have nothing more to say. When we use our spirit to pray, it functions as a shining lamp, searching all the parts of our soul. It may shine on our thoughts, but we refuse to have the Lord probe there. We may not say, "No, Lord! Don't touch there," but that is what we mean. The spirit may shine on our emotions, especially the sisters', but we close up, sometimes even weeping, begging the Lord not to touch that area. The same thing may happen with our will, especially the brothers'; if we close our will, the spirit cannot fulfill its function of shining. When we close the doors to the Lord's shining, we no longer have any words to pray.

When we pray properly, using our spirit, there is a lamp shining. If we sense it shining on our thoughts, we can say, "Lord, I open my mind to You. Shine in me. Expose my thoughts." In His light we confess our sins. When He shines on our emotions, we can open and confess what He reveals to be wrong. Then He will shine on our will, and we can open this room also to Him. As we open all these chambers one by one, the spirit will shine and we shall confess our sins. We can keep praying for a long time. The more we pray, the more we are enlightened. Our inward parts will all be thoroughly searched by the Lord. After such a time of prayer, we shall feel bright and transparent, filled with God. This is one aspect of the lamp, our spirit shining within.

The other aspect is that of the seven Spirits. The Spirit of God today is the seven lamps, shining on us in an intensified way. Many of us have experienced this intensified shining, far stronger than a simple prick of the conscience, condemning a wrong thought or wrong motive. What did not bother us in the past we can no longer do. If we open our mouth to tell a joke, the seven Spirits shine and our sentence is cut off in midair. If we begin to make some critical comments about a certain sister, the seven Spirits shine and our words fail. Even when we are off just a little, the Spirit is there as the light shining. (*Life Messages,* pp. 301-303)

Further Reading: Life Messages, chs. 68-70, 74-75

Enlightenment and inspiration: _____

Hymns, #395

1   O Jesus Christ, grow Thou in me,
     And all things else recede;
   My heart be daily nearer Thee,
     From sin be daily freed.

     Each day let Thy supporting might
       My weakness still embrace;
     My darkness vanish in Thy light,
       Thy life my death efface.

2   In Thy bright beams which on me fall,
     Fade every evil thought;
   That I am nothing, Thou art all,
     I would be daily taught.

3   More of Thy glory let me see,
     Thou Holy, Wise, and True;
   I would Thy living image be,
     In joy and sorrow too.

4   Fill me with gladness from above,
     Hold me by strength divine;
   Lord, let the glow of Thy great love
     Through all my being shine.

5   Make this poor self grow less and less,
     Be Thou my life and aim;
   Oh, make me daily through Thy grace
     More meet to bear Thy name.

Composition for prophecy with main point and
sub-points: _____

_____
_____
_____
_____
_____
_____
_____
_____
_____
_____
_____
_____
_____
_____
_____
_____
_____
_____
_____
_____
_____
_____
_____
_____
_____
_____
_____
_____
_____
_____
_____
_____
_____
_____
_____

Christel as the Son of Man
Walking in the Midst
of the Golden Lampstands

Scripture Reading: Rev. 1:12—2:1

Day 1 **I. Christ as the Son of Man is the High Priest, "clothed with a garment reaching to the feet, and girded about at the breasts with a golden girdle" (Rev. 1:13), to cherish the churches in His humanity and nourish them in His divinity:**

A. The Son of Man is in His humanity, the golden girdle signifies His divinity, and breasts are a sign of love:

1. Christ was girded at the loins, strengthened for the divine work (Exo. 28:4; Dan. 10:5) to produce the churches, but now He is girded about at the breasts, caring for the churches which He has produced by His love.

2. The golden girdle signifies Christ's divinity as His divine energy, and the breasts signify that this golden energy is exercised and motivated by and with His love to nourish the churches.

Day 2 B. Christ takes care of the churches in His humanity as the Son of Man to cherish them (Rev. 1:13a):

1. He dresses the lamps of the lampstands to make them proper, cherishing us that we may be happy, pleasant, and comfortable (Exo. 30:7; cf. Psa. 42:5, 11):

   a. The Lord's presence provides an atmosphere of tenderness and warmth to cherish our being, giving us rest, comfort, healing, cleansing, and encouragement.

   b. We can enjoy the cherishing atmosphere of the Lord's presence in the church to receive the nourishing supply of life (Eph. 5:29; cf. 1 Tim. 4:6; Eph. 4:11).

2. He trims the wicks of the lamps of the lampstand, cutting off all the negative things which frustrate our shining (Exo. 25:38):

   a. The charred part of the wick, the snuff, signifies things that are not according to God's purpose which need to be cut off, such as our flesh, our natural man, our self, and our old creation.

   b. He trims away all the differences among the churches (the wrongdoings, shortages, failures, and defects) so that they may be the same in essence, appearance, and expression (cf. 1 Cor. 1:10; 2 Cor. 12:18; Phil. 2:2).

Day 3   C. Christ takes care of the churches in His divinity with His divine love, signified by the golden girdle on His breasts, to nourish the churches (Rev. 1:13b):

1. He nourishes us with Himself as the all-inclusive Christ in His full ministry of three stages so that we may grow and mature in the divine life to be His overcomers to accomplish His eternal economy.

2. As the walking Christ, He gets to know the condition of each church, and as the speaking Spirit, He trims and fills the lampstands with fresh oil, the supply of the Spirit (Rev. 2:1, 7).

3. To participate in His move and enjoy His care, we must be in the churches.

Day 4   II. **The heavenly ancientness of the Lord is depicted by His head and hair being as white as white wool, as snow (Rev. 1:14a; Dan. 7:9; Job 15:10; cf. S. S. 5:11).**

III. **The Lord's seven eyes are like a flame of fire for watching, observing, searching, and judging by enlightening and infusing (Rev. 1:14b; 5:6; Dan. 10:6):**

A. Christ's eyes are for God's move and operation on earth, since seven is the number for completion in God's move.

B. The Lord's eyes being like a flame of fire is mainly for His judgment (Dan. 7:9-10; Rev. 2:18; 19:11-12).

Day 5   IV. **The Lord's feet are like shining bronze, as having been fired in a furnace, signifying that His perfect and bright walk qualifies Him to exercise divine judgment (Rev. 1:15a; Ezek. 1:7; Dan. 10:6).**

V. **The Lord's voice is like the sound of many waters (Rev. 1:15b; cf. 14:2), which is a tumultuous sound, the sound of the voice of the Almighty God (Ezek. 1:24; 43:2) in its seriousness and solemnity (cf. Rev. 10:3).**

VI. **Christ is the Holder of the bright messengers of the churches (1:16a, 20):**

A. The messengers are the spiritual ones in the churches, the ones who bear the responsibility of the testimony of Jesus.

B. The messengers, who are of the heavenly nature and in a heavenly position like stars, are those who have a fresh message from the Lord to His people (Rev. 2:1a).

C. Because the leading ones are in His right hand, there is no need for them to shrink back; Christ truly takes the responsibility for His testimony.

Day 6   VII. **Out of Christ's mouth proceeds a sharp two-edged sword, which is His discerning, judging, and slaying word for dealing with negative persons and things (1:16b; Heb. 4:12; Eph. 6:17).**

VIII. **Christ's face is as the sun shining in its power (cf. Dan. 10:6) for judging enlightenment to bring in the kingdom (Rev. 1:16c; 10:1; Matt. 17:2; cf. Mal. 4:2; Judg. 5:31; Matt. 13:43).**

IX. **Christ is the First and the Last, assuring us that He will never leave His work unfin-**

ished, and the living One for the churches
as the expression of His Body to be living,
fresh, and strong (Rev. 1:17-18a).

X. Christ has the keys of death and of Hades
(v. 18b):

A. Death is a collector and Hades is a keeper, but
Christ nullified death on the cross and over-
came Hades in His resurrection (2 Tim. 1:10;
Acts 2:24).

B. As long as we give the Lord the ground, the
opportunity, and the way to move and act
among us by our exercising to deny the self,
take up the cross, and lose our soul-life, death
and Hades will be under His control (Matt.
16:18, 21-26).

Morning Nourishment

Rev. **And I turned to see the voice that spoke with**
1:12 **me; and when I turned, I saw seven golden**
lampstands,
   13 **And in the midst of the lampstands One like the**
Son of Man, clothed with a garment reaching to
the feet, and girded about at the breasts with a
golden girdle.

Revelation 1 shows us how Christ cares for the churches. Revelation is a book of signs. A sign is a symbol with spiritual significance. The first sign in Revelation shows us Christ in His humanity as the High Priest, and the last sign is the New Jerusalem. As the Son of Man, Christ as the High Priest is taking care of all the churches as lampstands (1:12-13). On the one hand, He is cherishing the churches in His humanity; on the other hand, He is nourishing the churches in His divinity. The members of the vital groups have to learn these two things. When we visit people, invite them to our home, or contact them before and after the meetings, we must be one with Christ to cherish and nourish them. (*The Vital Groups,* p. 102)

Today's Reading

Christ is the best model of cherishing and nourishing as seen in Revelation 1. In verses 12 and 13 John said, "I turned to see the voice that spoke with me; and when I turned, I saw seven golden lampstands, and in the midst of the lampstands One like the Son of Man, clothed with a garment reaching to the feet, and girded about at the breasts with a golden girdle." This shows that Christ is taking care of the lampstands by being the Son of Man with a long garment. This garment is the priestly robe

(Exo. 28:33-35), which shows that Christ is our great High Priest.

He is also girded about at the breasts with a golden girdle. This girdle is a long piece of gold. The girdle and the gold are not two separate things. The girdle is the gold. The golden girdle is one piece of gold to become a belt. The Son of Man is in His humanity, and the golden girdle signifies His divinity. This golden girdle is on His breasts, and the breasts are a sign of love.

The priests in the Old Testament were girded at the loins for their ministry (Exo. 28:4). In Daniel 10:5 Christ also is girded at His loins, with fine gold. To be girded at the loins is to be strengthened for the work. Christ has finished His divine work in producing the churches. Now by His love He is caring for the churches which He has produced. This is why He is girded at the breasts. Today Christ is our High Priest taking care of His churches established by His labor. But now He takes care of the churches with the girdle not on His loins but on His breasts, signifying love. I hope we all could realize that in these days even among us, Christ is wearing a golden girdle on His breasts.

The golden girdle is a sign, signifying Christ's divinity becoming His energy. Christ's energy is totally His divinity. A piece of gold is now a girdle. The totality of Christ in His divinity has become a girdle. The golden girdle signifies Christ's divinity becoming His energy, and the breasts signify that this golden energy is exercised and motivated by His love. His divine energy is exercised by and with His love to nourish the churches. (*The Vital Groups,* pp. 105-106)

Further Reading: The Vital Groups, msg. 11; *Life-study of Revelation,* msg. 9

Enlightenment and inspiration: _____

_____

_____

_____

_____

Morning Nourishment

Rev. And in the midst of the lampstands One like the
1:13 Son of Man, clothed with a garment reaching to
the feet, and girded about at the breasts with a
golden girdle.

Eph. For no one ever hated his own flesh, but nour-
5:29 ishes and cherishes it, even as Christ also the
church,

30 Because we are members of His Body.

Heb. For we do not have a High Priest who cannot
4:15 be touched with the feeling of our weaknesses,
but One who has been tempted in all respects
like *us, yet* without sin.

I thank the Lord that today in His recovery He is the High Priest in His humanity. Hebrews 4 says that we do not have a High Priest who cannot be touched with the feeling of our weaknesses, but One who has been tempted in all respects like us, yet without sin (v. 15). Our Christ is the same as we are. He has been tempted in everything like us, so He can easily be touched with the feeling of our weaknesses. This means that He always sympathizes with our weaknesses in His humanity. He is the High Priest in His humanity taking care of us by cherishing us all the time. (*The Vital Groups,* p. 107)

Today's Reading

Christ takes care of the churches as the lampstands in His humanity as "the Son of Man" to cherish them (Rev. 1:13a). Christ as our High Priest takes care of the churches He has established first in His humanity to cherish the churches, to make the churches happy, pleasant, and comfortable.

He does this by dressing the lamps of the lampstand. The high priest in the Old Testament dressed the lamps of the lampstands every morning (Exo. 30:7). To dress the lamps is to make them proper.

Christ cares for the lampstands by trimming the wicks of the lamps of the lampstand, just as the priest did according to the type in the Old Testament (Exo. 25:38). When the wick was burned out it became charred and black, so the priest had to come to cut off the black part of the wick. This is what it means to snuff the wick so that the lamp may shine better. The charred part of the wick, the snuff, signifies things that are not according to God's purpose which need to be cut off, such as our flesh, our natural man, our self, and our old creation. All the lampstands are organic. They are living lampstands. Since each church is a living lampstand, each church has much feeling. A church with charred wicks will not feel comfortable.

About eight years ago, there was no feeling of happiness or pleasantness with the church in Anaheim. This was because of the black, burned out, charred wicks. But one day Christ as our High Priest came to dress the lamps of the lampstand, the church in Anaheim, by trimming the wicks to cut off all the black, charred wicks. This was a cherishing, to make the church in Anaheim happy, pleasant, and comfortable. There is no comparison between the way the church in Anaheim was eight years ago and the way it is today. Eight years ago it was full of burned, black wicks, with no shining. The saints felt unhappy, unpleasant, and uncomfortable. But one day the Lord Jesus as the High Priest in His humanity came to snuff all the negative things. Then we became happy, pleasant, and comfortable. This is Christ's taking care of the church in His humanity to dress the lamps of the church. (*The Vital Groups,* pp. 106-107)

Further Reading: The Vital Groups, msg. 11; *Life-study of Ephesians,* msg. 53

Enlightenment and inspiration: _____

_____

_____

_____

Morning Nourishment

Rev. ...To him who overcomes, to him I will give to eat
2:7 of the tree of life, which is in the Paradise of God.
17   ...To him who overcomes, to him I will give of the
     hidden manna....
3:20 Behold, I stand at the door and knock; if anyone
     hears My voice and opens the door, then I will
     come in to him and dine with him and he with Me.

Christ, as the High Priest, takes care of the churches as the lampstands in His divinity with His divine love, signified by the golden girdle on His breasts, to nourish the churches (Rev. 1:13b). Christ is not only human but also divine. He is the Son of Man wearing a golden girdle, signifying His divinity as His divine energy. His divinity as the divine energy nourishes the churches in many ways.

Revelation 2 and 3 reveal Christ's care for the lampstands. On the one hand, He trims the wicks of the church lamps, cutting away all the wrongdoings, shortages, failures, and defects mentioned in the seven epistles to the seven churches. Christ did the best trimming work in His humanity to cherish the churches. On the other hand, in each of these seven epistles, we see Christ's nourishing. (*The Vital Groups*, p. 107)

Today's Reading

In the first epistle to the church at Ephesus, Christ says, "To him who overcomes, to him I will give to eat of the tree of life, which is in the Paradise of God" (2:7). We may say that this is a prophecy referring to the kingdom age, in which the overcomers will enjoy Christ as the tree of life in God's Paradise. But if we do not enjoy Christ as the tree of life in the church life today, surely we will not participate in the tree of life in the kingdom age. According to my experience, today the church in Anaheim is a paradise to me. In this paradise I eat much of Christ as the tree of life every day. If I do not eat Christ here today, I will not eat Him in the kingdom age. I have to eat here first.

The Lord will give the overcomers in Pergamos to eat of the hidden manna (v. 17). In the Old Testament, a portion of manna was preserved in a golden pot concealed in the ark (Exo. 16:32-34; Heb. 9:4). Today we must enjoy the hidden Christ in God's golden divine nature. Then we will enjoy Christ as the hidden manna in the coming age. Also, the Lord will give us a white stone and a new name, signifying that we have become a transformed person to be material for God's building.

The Lord counseled the church in Laodicea to buy gold, white garments, and eyesalve to be saved from their degradation in lukewarmness (Rev. 3:18). He promised to dine with the ones who would open the door to Him (v. 20). We can see that this is the nourishing of Christ in His divinity exercised by and with His love.

He is also the High Priest with His divinity as the "energy belt" to nourish us with Himself as the all-inclusive Christ in His full ministry of three stages.

His nourishing the churches in His divinity is so that the churches may grow and mature in His divine life and become the overcomers in His sevenfold intensification.

Our Christ today is our High Priest. In His humanity He is easily touched with the feeling of our weaknesses. He sympathizes with our weakness because He was tempted in all respects like us. He is cherishing us in His humanity. Meanwhile, He is nourishing us in His divinity with all the positive aspects of His person revealed in the seven epistles to the seven churches in Revelation 2 and 3. He is taking care of the churches in the recovery in both ways. In His humanity He is cherishing us to make us proper so that we may be happy, pleasant, and comfortable. In His divinity He is nourishing us so that we may grow and mature in the divine life to be His overcomers to accomplish His eternal economy. (*The Vital Groups*, pp. 107-109)

Further Reading: The Vital Groups, msg. 11; *The Mending Ministry of John*, ch. 14

Enlightenment and inspiration: _____

_____

_____

Morning Nourishment

Rev. And His head and hair were as white as white wool,
1:14 as snow; and His eyes were like a flame of fire.
5:6   And I saw in the midst of the throne...a Lamb
      standing as having *just* been slain, having seven
      horns and seven eyes, which are the seven Spirits
      of God sent forth into all the earth.
Dan. His body also was like beryl, His face like the ap-
10:6 pearance of lightning, His eyes like torches of fire....

White hair [in Revelation 1:14] signifies great age (Job 15:10). The black hair with which the Lord is depicted in Song of Songs 5:11 signifies His unfading and everlasting strength, but the white hair with which He is depicted here signifies His ancientness.

Although Christ is ancient, He is not old. In this chapter we see that His head and His hair were white as wool and as snow. White wool issues from the nature of life, and white snow comes down from the sky, from heaven. Wool is not made white; it is born white, and its whiteness comes out of its nature. White wool is the color of Christ's nature. His ancientness is of His nature. Snow is white because it comes from heaven and contains no earthly dirt or stain. Hence, white wool, both here and in Daniel 7:9, signifies that the ancientness of Christ is of His nature, not of His becoming old, while white snow signifies that His ancientness is heavenly, not earthly. (*Life-study of Revelation*, pp. 104-105)

Today's Reading

In verse 14, we see that His eyes are as a flame of fire. In Song of Songs 5:12 the eyes of Christ are like doves. That is for the expression of His love. Here "His eyes" are "like a flame of fire." This is for Him to observe and search in His judging by enlightening. In this book His eyes are not two but seven (5:6). Seven is the number of completion in God's move. Hence, His eyes in this book are for God's operation. These seven eyes of

His are the "seven lamps of fire burning before the throne, which are the seven Spirits of God" (4:5; cf. Dan. 10:6). The "fire burning" equals the "flame of fire" and is for observing and searching. The seven Spirits of God which are sent forth into all the earth are also for God's move upon the earth. Thus, the eyes of Christ in this book are the seven Spirits of God for God's move and operation on earth today.

Christ's eyes are for watching, observing, searching, judging by enlightening, and infusing. We must experience all these different aspects of His eyes, especially the aspect of infusing. His eyes infuse us with all that He is. His infusing eyes are a flame of fire which is continually burning. This can be proved by our experience. Do not exercise your mind to understand this, but check with your experience. Since the day we were saved, Christ's eyes have been like a burning fire enlightening and infusing us. His eyes also stir us up to be hot. After Christ has looked at us, we can never be cold as we once were. By looking at us, He burns us and stirs us up in the Lord. Many times the Lord comes to us with His piercing eyes. Perhaps when we are trying to hide something from our wives, the Lord comes with seven shining eyes piercing into our being and exposing our true condition. I have had this kind of experience hundreds of times. When I was arguing with others, especially with my intimate ones, the shining eyes of Christ were upon me, and I could not go on speaking. His shining stopped my mouth.

The book of Revelation is a book with a judging nature. Fire is for divine judgment (1 Cor. 3:13; Heb. 6:8; 10:27). "Our God is also a consuming fire" (Heb. 12:29). His throne is like the fiery flame and its wheels as burning fire, and a fiery stream issues and comes forth from before Him (Dan. 7:9-10). All this is for judgment. The main significance of the Lord's eyes being as a flame of fire is for His judgment (2:18-23; 19:11-12). When He comes to take possession of the earth by exercising judgment over it, even His feet will be like pillars of fire (10:1). (*Life-study of Revelation*, pp. 105-106)

Further Reading: Life-study of Revelation, msg. 9

Enlightenment and inspiration: _____

_____

Morning Nourishment

Rev. And His feet were like shining bronze, as having
1:15 been fired in a furnace; and His voice was like
the sound of many waters.

16 And He had in His right hand seven stars....

2:1 ...These things says He who holds the seven stars
in His right hand, He who walks in the midst of
the seven golden lampstands.

The elders need to be the Lord's messengers as shining stars
(Rev. 2:1, 8, 12, 18, 3:1, 7, 14). A messenger is one that brings a
message from the Lord to His people. Every elder should be one
that always speaks for the Lord and brings some word, some
message, from the Lord. The elders also should be the shining
stars....An elder must be apt to teach (1 Tim. 3:2). To be apt to
teach is to bring a word, a message, from the Lord to His people.
One who does this is a messenger. Such a one is not simply
speaking with his mouth, but also shining by what he does and
what he is. The messenger himself is a star. A star simply shines.
On the one hand, we need to be messengers, and on the other
hand, we need to be the shining stars. (*Elders' Training,
Book 11: The Eldership and the God-ordained Way (3)*, p. 13)

Today's Reading

[In Revelation 1:15], feet signify the walk. In typology,
bronze signifies divine judgment (Exo. 27:1-6). When Christ
was on earth, His earthly walk and daily walk were tried and
tested. Because His walk was tested, He came out shining....His perfect and bright walk qualifies Him to exercise
divine judgment.

Verse 16 says, "He had in His right hand seven stars." As
verse 20 makes clear, "the seven stars are the messengers of
the seven churches." The messengers are the spiritual ones in
the churches bearing the responsibility of the testimony of
Jesus. Like stars, they should be of the heavenly nature and in
a heavenly position. In the Acts and the Epistles the elders

were the leading ones in the operation of the local churches (Acts 14:23; 20:17; Titus 1:5). The eldership is somewhat official, and, as we have seen, at the time this book was written the offices in the churches had deteriorated in the degradation of the church. In this book the Lord calls our attention back to spiritual reality. Hence, it emphasizes the messengers of the churches rather than the elders. The office of the elders is easily perceived, but the believers need to see the importance of the spiritual and heavenly reality of the messengers for the proper church life to bear the testimony of Jesus in the darkness of the church's degradation.

Both the lampstands and the stars are for shining in the night. A lampstand representing a local church is a collective unit, whereas a star representing a messenger of a local church is an individual entity. In the dark night of the church's degradation, there is the need of the shining both of the collective churches and of the individual messengers. As Christ walks among the churches, He holds the leading ones in His right hand. How comforting this is! The leading ones must praise Him that they are in His hands and that He is holding them. Since the leading ones are in His hands, there is no need for them to shrink back, to be weak, or to be mistaken. Christ truly takes the responsibility for His testimony.

In the book of Revelation there are no elders in the churches; rather, there are messengers. At the time this book was written, the church had become degraded. Hence, in Revelation, the Lord repudiates all formalities. Being an elder may be somewhat legal or formal. Do not aspire to be an elder; desire to be a shining star. Do not be one with a mere position—be a shining star. Both the lampstand and the stars shine at night. Both the church and the leading ones in the churches must shine. All the leading ones must be stars. (*Life-study of Revelation,* pp. 106-108)

Further Reading: Life-study of Revelation, msg. 9; *Elders' Training, Book 11: The Eldership and the God-ordained Way (3),* ch. 1

Enlightenment and inspiration: _____

_____

Morning Nourishment

Rev. ...And out of His mouth proceeded a sharp two-
1:16 edged sword; and His face *shone* as the sun shines
in its power.
   17 And when I saw Him, I fell at His feet as dead; and
He placed His right hand on me, saying, Do not
fear; I am the First and the Last
   18 And the living One; and I became dead, and behold, I am living forever and ever; and I have the
keys of death and of Hades.

In Revelation 1:16 we are told that "out of His mouth
proceeded a sharp two-edged sword."...This is His discerning,
judging, and slaying word (Heb. 4:12; Eph. 6:17). The "words of
grace" [Luke 4:22] are for His supply of grace to His favored
ones, whereas the "sharp two-edged sword" is for His dealing
with negative persons and things. We often say that the Spirit
speaks to the churches. Remember that the speaking Spirit
today is just this Christ who speaks with a two-edged sword.
There is judgment here, and we all have experienced this.
Because of the church's degradation, we all need a certain
amount of judgment....In the Lord's recovery today we have
One who is walking in our midst. He watches over us with His
seven burning eyes, and out of His mouth proceeds a sharp
two-edged sword. (*Life-study of Revelation*, pp. 108-109)

Today's Reading

In verse 16 we are also told that "His face shone as the sun
shines in its power,"...as in Daniel 10:6, for the judging enlightenment to bring in the kingdom. When He was transfigured and
His face shone as the sun, that was His coming in the kingdom
(Matt. 16:28—17:2). When He comes to take over the earth for
the kingdom, His face will be as the sun (10:1).

[In verse 17], Christ is not only the First and the Last, but
also the beginning and the ending. This assures us that, having
started the church life, He will surely accomplish it. He will

never leave His work unfinished. All the local churches must believe that the Lord Jesus is the beginning and the ending. He will accomplish what He has begun in His recovery.

In verse 18 we see that the Lord is "the living One," the One who "became dead" and who is "living for ever and ever." The very Christ who walks in the midst of the churches, who is the Head of the churches and to whom the churches belong, is the living One full of life. Hence, the churches as His Body should also be living and full of life.

In verse 18 the Lord also said, "I have the keys of death and of Hades." Due to the fall and sin of man, death came in and is now working on earth to gather up all the sinful people. Death resembles a dustpan used to collect the dust from the floor, and Hades resembles a trash can. Whatever the dustpan collects is put into the trash can. Thus, death is a collector and Hades is a keeper. In the church life today are we still subject to death and Hades? No! Christ abolished death on the cross and overcame Hades in His resurrection. Although Hades tried its best to hold Him, it was powerless to do it (Acts 2:24). With Him, death has no sting and Hades has no power. But what about us? It must be the same. In the church life, the keys of death and Hades are in His hand. It is impossible for us to deal with death; we simply do not have the ability to handle it. Whenever death enters, it will deaden many. But as long as we give the Lord Jesus the ground, the opportunity, and the free way to move and act among us, both death and Hades will be under His control. However, whenever the Lord Jesus does not have the ground in the church, death immediately becomes prevailing and Hades becomes powerful to hold the dead ones. Praise the Lord that Christ has the keys of death and Hades. Death is subject to Him and Hades is under His control. Hallelujah! (*Life-study of Revelation*, pp. 110-111)

Further Reading: Life-study of Revelation, msg. 9; *The Exercise of the Kingdom for the Building Up of the Church,* msgs. 3, 5

Enlightenment and inspiration: _____

_____

_____

_____

Hymns, #1122

1 "Seven Spirits" of our God—
   Lo, the age has now been turned
   To the Spirit with the Son.
   For the churches He's concerned.

   Come, O seven Spirits, come,
   Thy recovery work be done!
   Burn and search us thoroughly,
   All the churches are for Thee.
     Burn us, search us,
   All the churches are for Thee!

2 Sevenfold the Spirit is
   For the deadness of the church,
   That the saints may turn and live,
   That the Lord may burn and search.

3 Now the Spirit of our God
   Has become intensified:
   'Tis not one but sevenfold
   That the church may be supplied!

4 Now the seven Spirits are
   Seven lamps of burning fire,
   Not to teach us, but to burn,
   Satisfying God's desire.

5 See the seven Spirits now—
   Seven piercing, searching eyes.
   In the church exposing us,
   All the church He purifies.

6 Seven Spirits doth the Lord
   For the churches now employ;
   All those in the local church
   May this Spirit now enjoy.

Composition for prophecy with main point and sub-points: _____

_____

_____

_____

_____

_____

_____

_____

_____

_____

_____

_____

_____

_____

_____

_____

_____

_____

_____

_____

_____

_____

_____

_____

_____

_____

_____

_____

_____

_____

_____

_____

_____

Reading Schedule for the Recovery Version of the New Testament with Footnotes

Wk.	Lord's Day	Monday	Tuesday	Wednesday	Thursday	Friday	Saturday
1	☐ Matt 1:1-2	☐ 1:3-7	☐ 1:8-17	☐ 1:18-25	☐ 2:1-23	☐ 3:1-6	☐ 3:7-17
2	☐ 4:1-11	☐ 4:12-25	☐ 5:1-4	☐ 5:5-12	☐ 5:13-20	☐ 5:21-26	☐ 5:27-48
3	☐ 6:1-8	☐ 6:9-18	☐ 6:19-34	☐ 7:1-12	☐ 7:13-29	☐ 8:1-13	☐ 8:14-22
4	☐ 8:23-34	☐ 9:1-13	☐ 9:14-17	☐ 9:18-34	☐ 9:35—10:5	☐ 10:6-25	☐ 10:26-42
5	☐ 11:1-15	☐ 11:16-27	☐ 12:1-14	☐ 12:15-32	☐ 12:33-42	☐ 12:43—13:2	☐ 13:3-12
6	☐ 13:13-30	☐ 13:31-43	☐ 13:44-58	☐ 14:1-13	☐ 14:14-21	☐ 14:22-36	☐ 15:1-20
7	☐ 15:21-31	☐ 15:32-39	☐ 16:1-12	☐ 16:13-20	☐ 16:21-28	☐ 17:1-13	☐ 17:14-27
8	☐ 18:1-14	☐ 18:15-22	☐ 18:23-35	☐ 19:1-15	☐ 19:16-30	☐ 20:1-16	☐ 20:17-34
9	☐ 21:1-11	☐ 21:21-22	☐ 21:23-32	☐ 21:33-46	☐ 22:1-22	☐ 22:23-33	☐ 22:34-46
10	☐ 23:1-12	☐ 23:13-39	☐ 24:1-14	☐ 24:15-31	☐ 24:32-51	☐ 25:1-13	☐ 25:14-30
11	☐ 25:31-46	☐ 26:1-16	☐ 26:17-35	☐ 26:36-46	☐ 26:47-64	☐ 26:65-75	☐ 27:1-26
12	☐ 27:27-44	☐ 27:45-56	☐ 27:57—28:15	☐ 28:16-20	☐ Mark 1:1	☐ 1:2-6	☐ 1:7-13
13	☐ 1:14-28	☐ 1:29-45	☐ 2:1-12	☐ 2:13-28	☐ 3:1-19	☐ 3:20-35	☐ 4:1-25
14	☐ 4:26-41	☐ 5:1-20	☐ 5:21-43	☐ 6:1-29	☐ 6:30-56	☐ 7:1-23	☐ 7:24-37
15	☐ 8:1-26	☐ 8:27—9:1	☐ 9:2-29	☐ 9:30-50	☐ 10:1-16	☐ 10:17-34	☐ 10:35-52
16	☐ 11:1-16	☐ 11:17-33	☐ 12:1-27	☐ 12:28-44	☐ 13:1-13	☐ 13:14-37	☐ 14:1-26
17	☐ 14:27-52	☐ 14:53-72	☐ 15:1-15	☐ 15:16-47	☐ 16:1-8	☐ 16:9-20	☐ Luke 1:1-4
18	☐ 1:5-25	☐ 1:26-46	☐ 1:47-56	☐ 1:57-80	☐ 2:1-8	☐ 2:9-20	☐ 2:21-39
19	☐ 2:40-52	☐ 3:1-20	☐ 3:21-38	☐ 4:1-13	☐ 4:14-30	☐ 4:31-44	☐ 5:1-26
20	☐ 5:27—6:16	☐ 6:17-38	☐ 6:39-49	☐ 7:1-17	☐ 7:18-23	☐ 7:24-35	☐ 7:36-50
21	☐ 8:1-15	☐ 8:16-25	☐ 8:26-39	☐ 8:40-56	☐ 9:1-17	☐ 9:18-26	☐ 9:27-36
22	☐ 9:37-50	☐ 9:51-62	☐ 10:1-11	☐ 10:12-24	☐ 10:25-37	☐ 10:38-42	☐ 11:1-13
23	☐ 11:14-26	☐ 11:27-36	☐ 11:37-54	☐ 12:1-12	☐ 12:13-21	☐ 12:22-34	☐ 12:35-48
24	☐ 12:49-59	☐ 13:1-9	☐ 13:10-17	☐ 13:18-30	☐ 13:31—14:6	☐ 14:7-14	☐ 14:15-24
25	☐ 14:25-35	☐ 15:1-10	☐ 15:11-21	☐ 15:22-32	☐ 16:1-13	☐ 16:14-22	☐ 16:23-31
26	☐ 17:1-19	☐ 17:20-37	☐ 18:1-14	☐ 18:15-30	☐ 18:31-43	☐ 19:1-10	☐ 19:11-27

Reading Schedule for the Recovery Version of the New Testament with Footnotes

Wk.	Lord's Day	Monday	Tuesday	Wednesday	Thursday	Friday	Saturday
27	☐ Luke 19:28-48	☐ 20:1-19	☐ 20:20-38	☐ 20:39—21:4	☐ 21:5-27	☐ 21:28-38	☐ 22:1-20
28	☐ 22:21-38	☐ 22:39-54	☐ 22:55-71	☐ 23:1-43	☐ 23:44-56	☐ 24:1-12	☐ 24:13-35
29	☐ 24:36-53	☐ John 1:1-13	☐ 1:14-18	☐ 1:19-34	☐ 1:35-51	☐ 2:1-11	☐ 2:12-22
30	☐ 2:23—3:13	☐ 3:14-21	☐ 3:22-36	☐ 4:1-14	☐ 4:15-26	☐ 4:27-42	☐ 4:43-54
31	☐ 5:1-16	☐ 5:17-30	☐ 5:31-47	☐ 6:1-15	☐ 6:16-31	☐ 6:32-51	☐ 6:52-71
32	☐ 7:1-9	☐ 7:10-24	☐ 7:25-36	☐ 7:37-52	☐ 8:1-11	☐ 8:12-27	☐ 8:28-44
33	☐ 8:45-59	☐ 9:1-13	☐ 9:14-34	☐ 9:35—10:9	☐ 10:10-30	☐ 10:42—11:4	☐ 11:5-22
34	☐ 11:23-40	☐ 11:41-57	☐ 12:1-11	☐ 12:12-24	☐ 12:25-36	☐ 12:37-50	☐ 13:1-11
35	☐ 13:12-30	☐ 13:31-38	☐ 14:1-6	☐ 14:7-20	☐ 14:21-31	☐ 15:1-11	☐ 15:12-27
36	☐ 16:1-15	☐ 16:16-33	☐ 17:1-5	☐ 17:6-13	☐ 17:14-24	☐ 17:25—18:11	☐ 18:12-27
37	☐ 18:28-40	☐ 19:1-16	☐ 19:17-30	☐ 19:31-42	☐ 20:1-13	☐ 20:14-18	☐ 20:19-22
38	☐ 20:23-31	☐ 21:1-14	☐ 21:15-22	☐ 21:23-25	☐ Acts 1:1-8	☐ 1:9-14	☐ 1:15-26
39	☐ 2:1-13	☐ 2:14-21	☐ 2:22-36	☐ 2:37-41	☐ 2:42-47	☐ 3:1-18	☐ 3:19—4:22
40	☐ 4:23-37	☐ 5:1-16	☐ 5:17-32	☐ 5:33-42	☐ 6:1—7:1	☐ 7:2-29	☐ 7:30-60
41	☐ 8:1-13	☐ 8:14-25	☐ 8:26-40	☐ 9:1-19	☐ 9:20-43	☐ 10:1-16	☐ 10:17-33
42	☐ 10:34-48	☐ 11:1-18	☐ 11:19-30	☐ 12:1-25	☐ 13:1-12	☐ 13:13-43	☐ 13:44—14:5
43	☐ 14:6-28	☐ 15:1-12	☐ 15:13-34	☐ 15:35—16:5	☐ 16:6-18	☐ 16:19-40	☐ 17:1-18
44	☐ 17:19-34	☐ 18:1-17	☐ 18:18-28	☐ 19:1-20	☐ 19:21-41	☐ 20:1-12	☐ 20:13-38
45	☐ 21:1-14	☐ 21:15-26	☐ 21:27-40	☐ 22:1-21	☐ 22:22-29	☐ 22:30—23:11	☐ 23:12-15
46	☐ 23:16-30	☐ 23:31—24:21	☐ 24:22—25:5	☐ 25:6-27	☐ 26:1-13	☐ 26:14-32	☐ 27:1-26
47	☐ 27:27—28:10	☐ 28:11-22	☐ 28:23-31	☐ Rom 1:1-2	☐ 1:3-7	☐ 1:8-17	☐ 1:18-25
48	☐ 1:26—2:10	☐ 2:11-29	☐ 3:1-20	☐ 3:21-31	☐ 4:1-12	☐ 4:13-25	☐ 5:1-11
49	☐ 5:12-17	☐ 5:18—6:5	☐ 6:6-11	☐ 6:12-23	☐ 7:1-12	☐ 7:13-25	☐ 8:1-2
50	☐ 8:4-6	☐ 8:7-13	☐ 8:14-25	☐ 8:26-39	☐ 9:1-18	☐ 9:19—10:3	☐ 10:4-15
51	☐ 10:16—11:10	☐ 11:11-22	☐ 11:23-36	☐ 12:1-3	☐ 12:4-21	☐ 13:1-14	☐ 14:1-12
52	☐ 14:13-23	☐ 15:1-13	☐ 15:14-33	☐ 16:1-5	☐ 16:6-24	☐ 16:25-27	☐ I Cor 1:1-4

Reading Schedule for the Recovery Version of the New Testament with Footnotes

Wk.	Lord's Day	Monday	Tuesday	Wednesday	Thursday	Friday	Saturday
53	☐ I Cor 1:5-9	☐ 1:10-17	☐ 1:18-31	☐ 2:1-5	☐ 2:6-10	☐ 2:11-16	☐ 3:1-9
54	☐ 3:10-13	☐ 3:14-23	☐ 4:1-9	☐ 4:10-21	☐ 5:1-13	☐ 6:1-11	☐ 6:12-20
55	☐ 7:1-16	☐ 7:17-24	☐ 7:25-40	☐ 8:1-13	☐ 9:1-15	☐ 9:16-27	☐ 10:1-4
56	☐ 10:5-13	☐ 10:14-33	☐ 11:1-6	☐ 11:7-16	☐ 11:17-26	☐ 11:27-34	☐ 12:1-11
57	☐ 12:12-22	☐ 12:23-31	☐ 13:1-13	☐ 14:1-12	☐ 14:13-25	☐ 14:26-33	☐ 14:34-40
58	☐ 15:1-19	☐ 15:20-28	☐ 15:29-34	☐ 15:35-49	☐ 15:50-58	☐ 16:1-9	☐ 16:10-24
59	☐ II Cor 1:1-4	☐ 1:5-14	☐ 1:15-22	☐ 1:23—2:11	☐ 2:12-17	☐ 3:1-6	☐ 3:7-11
60	☐ 3:12-18	☐ 4:1-6	☐ 4:7-12	☐ 4:13-18	☐ 5:1-8	☐ 5:9-15	☐ 5:16-21
61	☐ 6:1-13	☐ 6:14—7:4	☐ 7:5-16	☐ 8:1-15	☐ 8:16-24	☐ 9:1-15	☐ 10:1-6
62	☐ 10:7-18	☐ 11:1-15	☐ 11:16-33	☐ 12:1-10	☐ 12:11-21	☐ 13:1-10	☐ 13:11-14
63	☐ Gal 1:1-5	☐ 1:6-14	☐ 1:15-24	☐ 2:1-13	☐ 2:14-21	☐ 3:1-4	☐ 3:5-14
64	☐ 3:15-22	☐ 3:23-29	☐ 4:1-7	☐ 4:8-20	☐ 4:21-31	☐ 5:1-12	☐ 5:13-21
65	☐ 5:22-26	☐ 6:1-10	☐ 6:11-15	☐ 6:16-18	☐ Eph 1:1-3	☐ 1:4-6	☐ 1:7-10
66	☐ 1:11-14	☐ 1:15-18	☐ 1:19-23	☐ 2:1-5	☐ 2:6-10	☐ 2:11-14	☐ 2:15-18
67	☐ 2:19-22	☐ 3:1-7	☐ 3:8-13	☐ 3:14-18	☐ 3:19-21	☐ 4:1-4	☐ 4:5-10
68	☐ 4:11-16	☐ 4:17-24	☐ 4:25-32	☐ 5:1-10	☐ 5:11-21	☐ 5:22-26	☐ 5:27-33
69	☐ 6:1-9	☐ 6:10-14	☐ 6:15-18	☐ 6:19-24	☐ Phil 1:1-7	☐ 1:8-18	☐ 1:19-26
70	☐ 1:29—2:4	☐ 2:5-11	☐ 2:12-16	☐ 2:17-30	☐ 3:1-6`	☐ 3:7-11	☐ 3:12-16
71	☐ 3:17-21	☐ 4:1-9	☐ 4:10-23	☐ Col 1:1-8	☐ 1:9-13	☐ 1:14-23	☐ 1:24-29
72	☐ 2:1-7	☐ 2:8-15	☐ 2:16-23	☐ 3:1-4	☐ 3:5-15	☐ 3:16-25	☐ 4:1-18
73	☐ I Thes 1:1-3	☐ 1:4-10	☐ 2:1-12	☐ 2:13—3:5	☐ 3:6-13	☐ 4:1-10	☐ 4:11—5:11
74	☐ 5:12-28	☐ II Thes 1:1-12	☐ 2:1-17	☐ 3:1-18	☐ I Tim 1:1-2	☐ 1:3-4	☐ 1:5-14
75	☐ 1:15-20	☐ 2:1-7	☐ 2:8-15	☐ 3:1-13	☐ 3:14—4:5	☐ 4:6-16	☐ 5:1-25
76	☐ 6:1-10	☐ 6:11-21	☐ II Tim 1:1-10	☐ 1:11-18	☐ 2:1-15	☐ 2:16-26	☐ 3:1-13
77	☐ 3:14—4:8	☐ 4:9-22	☐ Titus 1:1-4	☐ 1:5-16	☐ 2:1-15	☐ 3:1-8	☐ 3:9-15
78	☐ Philem 1:1-11	☐ 1:12-25	☐ Heb 1:1-2	☐ 1:3-5	☐ 1:6-14	☐ 2:1-9	☐ 2:10-18

Reading Schedule for the Recovery Version of the New Testament with Footnotes

Wk.	Lord's Day	Monday	Tuesday	Wednesday	Thursday	Friday	Saturday
79	☐ Heb 3:1-6	☐ 3:7-19	☐ 4:1-9	☐ 4:10-13	☐ 4:14-16	☐ 5:1-10	☐ 5:11—6:3
80	☐ 6:4-8	☐ 6:9-20	☐ 7:1-10	☐ 7:11-28	☐ 8:1-6	☐ 8:7-13	☐ 9:1-4
81	☐ 9:5-14	☐ 9:15-28	☐ 10:1-18	☐ 10:19-28	☐ 10:29-39	☐ 11:1-6	☐ 11:7-19
82	☐ 11:20-31	☐ 11:32-40	☐ 12:1-2	☐ 12:3-13	☐ 12:14-17	☐ 12:18-26	☐ 12:27-29
83	☐ 13:1-7	☐ 13:8-12	☐ 13:13-15	☐ 13:16-25	☐ James 1:1-8	☐ 1:9-18	☐ 1:19-27
84	☐ 2:1-13	☐ 2:14-26	☐ 3:1-18	☐ 4:1-10	☐ 4:11-17	☐ 5:1-12	☐ 5:13-20
85	☐ I Pet 1:1-2	☐ 1:3-4	☐ 1:5	☐ 1:6-9	☐ 1:10-12	☐ 1:13-17	☐ 1:18-25
86	☐ 2:1-3	☐ 2:4-8	☐ 2:9-17	☐ 2:18-25	☐ 3:1-13	☐ 3:14-22	☐ 4:1-6
87	☐ 4:7-16	☐ 4:17-19	☐ 5:1-4	☐ 5:5-9	☐ 5:10-14	☐ II Pet 1:1-2	☐ 1:3-4
88	☐ 1:5-8	☐ 1:9-11	☐ 1:12-18	☐ 1:19-21	☐ 2:1-3	☐ 2:4-11	☐ 2:12-22
89	☐ 3:1-6	☐ 3:7-9	☐ 3:10-12	☐ 3:13-15	☐ 3:16	☐ 3:17-18	☐ I John 1:1-2
90	☐ 1:3-4	☐ 1:5	☐ 1:6	☐ 1:7	☐ 1:8-10	☐ 2:1-2	☐ 2:3-11
91	☐ 2:12-14	☐ 2:15-19	☐ 2:20-23	☐ 2:24-27	☐ 2:28-29	☐ 3:1-5	☐ 3:6-10
92	☐ 3:11-18	☐ 3:19-24	☐ 4:1-6	☐ 4:7-11	☐ 4:12-15	☐ 4:16—5:3	☐ 5:4-13
93	☐ 5:14-17	☐ 5:18-21	☐ II John 1:1-3	☐ 1:4-9	☐ 1:10-13	☐ III John 1:1-6	☐ 1:7-14
94	☐ Jude 1:1-4	☐ 1:5-10	☐ 1:11-19	☐ 1:20-25	☐ Rev 1:1-3	☐ 1:4-6	☐ 1:7-11
95	☐ 1:12-13	☐ 1:14-16	☐ 1:17-20	☐ 2:1-6	☐ 2:7	☐ 2:8-9	☐ 2:10-11
96	☐ 2:12-14	☐ 2:15-17	☐ 2:18-23	☐ 2:24-29	☐ 3:1-3	☐ 3:4-6	☐ 3:7-9
97	☐ 3:10-13	☐ 3:14-18	☐ 3:19-22	☐ 4:1-5	☐ 4:6-7	☐ 4:8-11	☐ 5:1-6
98	☐ 5:7-14	☐ 6:1-8	☐ 6:9-17	☐ 7:1-8	☐ 7:9-17	☐ 8:1-6	☐ 8:7-12
99	☐ 8:13—9:11	☐ 9:12-21	☐ 10:1-4	☐ 10:5-11	☐ 11:1-4	☐ 11:5-14	☐ 11:15-19
100	☐ 12:1-4	☐ 12:5-9	☐ 12:10-18	☐ 13:1-10	☐ 13:11-18	☐ 14:1-5	☐ 14:6-12
101	☐ 14:13-20	☐ 15:1-8	☐ 16:1-12	☐ 16:13-21	☐ 17:1-6	☐ 17:7-18	☐ 18:1-8
102	☐ 18:9—19:4	☐ 19:5-10	☐ 19:11-16	☐ 19:17-21	☐ 20:1-6	☐ 20:7-10	☐ 20:11-15
103	☐ 21:1	☐ 21:2	☐ 21:3-8	☐ 21:9-13	☐ 21:14-18	☐ 21:19-21	☐ 21:22-27
104	☐ 22:1	☐ 22:2	☐ 22:3-11	☐ 22:12-15	☐ 22:16-17	☐ 22:18-21	☐

Week 1 — Day 1

Today's verses

Rev. 1:1 The revelation of Jesus Christ which God gave to Him to show to His slaves the things that must quickly take place; and He made it known by signs, sending it by His angel to His slave John.

12 ...And when I turned, I saw seven golden lampstands.

21:2 And I saw the holy city, New Jerusalem, coming down out of heaven from God....

5-6 ...Write, for these words are faithful and true. And He said to me, They have come to pass....

_____
Date

Week 1 — Day 2

Today's verses

Rev. 14:15 ...Send forth Your sickle and reap, for the hour to reap has come because the harvest of the earth is ripe.

21:1-2 And I saw a new heaven and a new earth; for the first heaven and the first earth passed away, and the sea is no more. And I saw the holy city, New Jerusalem, coming down out of heaven from God, prepared as a bride adorned for her husband.

_____
Date

Week 1 — Day 3

Today's verses

Rev. 22:1-2 And he showed me a river of water of life, bright as crystal, proceeding out of the throne of God and of the Lamb in the middle of its street. And on this side and on that side of the river was the tree of life....

14 Blessed are those who wash their robes that they may have right to the tree of life and may enter by the gates into the city.

_____
Date

Week 1 — Day 4

Today's verses

Rev. 1:18 And the living One; and I became dead, and behold, I am living forever and ever; and I have the keys of death and of Hades.

22:13 I am the Alpha and the Omega, the First and the Last, the Beginning and the End.

_____
Date

Week 1 — Day 5

Today's verses

Rev. 3:1 And to the messenger of the church in Sardis write: These things says He who has the seven Spirits of God....

4:5 ...And there were seven lamps of fire burning before the throne, which are the seven Spirits of God.

5:6 And I saw in the midst of the throne...a Lamb standing as having just been slain, having seven horns and seven eyes, which are the seven Spirits of God sent forth into all the earth.

_____
Date

Week 1 — Day 6

Today's verses

Rev. 3:3 ...If therefore you will not watch, I will come as a thief, and you shall by no means know at what hour I will come upon you.

5:5 And one of the elders said to me, Do not weep; behold, the Lion of the tribe of Judah, the Root of David, has overcome so that He may open the scroll and its seven seals.

_____
Date

Week 2 — Day 4

Today's verses

Rev. And He is clothed with a garment dipped
19:13 in blood; and His name is called the
Word of God.

14 And the armies which are in heaven followed Him on white horses, dressed in
fine linen, white *and* clean.

15 And out of His mouth proceeds a sharp
sword, that with it He might smite the
nations; and He will shepherd them with
an iron rod; and He treads the winepress
of the fury of the wrath of God the Almighty.

_____
Date

Week 2 — Day 5

Today's verses

Eph. And receive the helmet of salvation and
6:17 the sword of the Spirit, which *Spirit* is the
word of God.

Heb. For the word of God is living and opera-
4:12 tive and sharper than any two-edged
sword, and piercing even to the dividing
of soul and spirit and of joints and marrow, and able to discern the thoughts and
intentions of the heart.

_____
Date

Week 2 — Day 6

Today's verses

Rev. And she brought forth a son, a man-child,
12:5 who is to shepherd all the nations with
an iron rod; and her child was caught up
to God and to His throne.

19:7 Let us rejoice and exult, and let us give
the glory to Him, for the marriage of the
Lamb has come, and His wife has made
herself ready.

10 ...I am your fellow slave and *a fellow
slave* of your brothers who have the testimony of Jesus. Worship God. For the
testimony of Jesus is the spirit of the
prophecy.

_____
Date

Week 2 — Day 1

Today's verses

Rev. The revelation of Jesus Christ which God
1:1-2 gave to Him to show to His slaves the
things that must quickly take place; and
He made *it* known by signs, sending *it* by
His angel to His slave John, who testified
the word of God and the testimony of
Jesus Christ, *even* all that he saw.

6:9 And when He opened the fifth seal, I saw
underneath the altar the souls of those
who had been slain because of the word
of God and because of the testimony
which they had.

_____
Date

Week 2 — Day 2

Today's verses

Exo. And when Moses came down from
34:29 Mount Sinai...Moses did not know that
the skin of his face shone by reason of His
speaking with him.

Psa. Cause Your face to shine on Your servant,
119:135 and teach me Your statutes.

2 Cor. But whenever *their heart* turns to the
3:16 Lord, the veil is taken away.

18 But we all with unveiled face, beholding
and reflecting like a mirror the glory of
the Lord, are being transformed into the
same image from glory to glory, even as
from the Lord Spirit.

_____
Date

Week 2 — Day 3

Today's verses

S. S. O you who dwell in the gardens, *my*
8:13 companions listen for your voice; let me
hear *it*.

Psa. Your statutes have become my songs of
119:54 praise in the house of my pilgrimage.

Col. Let the word of Christ dwell in you richly
3:16 in all wisdom, teaching and admonishing
one another with psalms *and* hymns *and*
spiritual songs, singing with grace in your
hearts to God.

_____
Date

Week 3 — Day 1
Today's verses

Matt. 28:19 Go therefore and disciple all the nations, baptizing them into the name of the Father and of the Son and of the Holy Spirit.

Date _____

Week 3 — Day 2
Today's verses

Rev. 1:4-5 ...Grace to you and peace from Him who is and who was and who is coming, and from the seven Spirits who are before His throne, and from Jesus Christ, the faithful Witness, the Firstborn of the dead, and the Ruler of the kings of the earth....

Eph. 1:4-5 Even as He chose us in Him,...predestinating us unto sonship through Jesus Christ to Himself, according to the good pleasure of His will.

7 In whom we have redemption....

13 ...In Him also believing, you were sealed with the Holy Spirit of the promise.

Date _____

Week 3 — Day 3
Today's verses

Rev. 22:17 And the Spirit and the bride say, Come!...

3:22 He who has an ear, let him hear what the Spirit says to the churches.

Date _____

Week 3 — Day 4
Today's verses

Rev. 3:1 ...These things says He who has the seven Spirits of God....

4:5 ...And *there were* seven lamps of fire burning before the throne, which are the seven Spirits of God.

5:6 And I saw...a Lamb standing as having *just* been slain, having seven horns and seven eyes, which are the seven Spirits of God sent forth into all the earth.

Date _____

Week 3 — Day 5
Today's verses

Rev. 21:18 And the building work of its wall was jasper; and the city was pure gold, like clear glass.

19 The foundations of the wall of the city were adorned with every precious stone....

21 And the twelve gates were twelve pearls....

Date _____

Week 3 — Day 6
Today's verses

John 4:14 But whoever drinks of the water that I will give him shall by no means thirst forever; but the water that I will give him will become in him a fountain of water gushing up into eternal life.

Rev. 7:17 For the Lamb who is in the midst of the throne will shepherd them and guide them to springs of waters of life....

21:6 ...I will give to him who thirsts from the spring of the water of life freely.

Date _____

Week 4 — Day 4   Today's verses

Rev. 5:1 And I saw on the right hand of Him who sits upon the throne a scroll written within and on the back, sealed up with seven seals.

Matt. 24:33 So also you, when you see all these things, know that it is near, at the doors.

2 Pet. 1:19 And we have the prophetic word made more firm, to which you do well to give heed as to a lamp shining in a dark place, until the day dawns and the morning star rises in your hearts.

_____
Date

Week 4 — Day 5   Today's verses

Rev. 3:10 Because you have kept the word of My endurance, I also will keep you out of the hour of trial, which is about to come on the whole inhabited earth, to try them who dwell on the earth.

22:20 He who testifies these things says, Yes, I come quickly. Amen. Come, Lord Jesus!

2 Tim. 4:8 Henceforth there is laid up for me the crown of righteousness, with which the Lord, the righteous Judge, will recompense me in that day, and not only me but also all those who have loved His appearing.

_____
Date

Week 4 — Day 6   Today's verses

Luke 21:34 But take heed to yourselves lest perhaps your hearts be weighed down with debauchery and drunkenness and the anxieties of life, and that day come upon you suddenly as a snare.

35 For it will come in upon all those dwelling on the face of all the earth.

Phil. 3:20 For our commonwealth exists in the heavens, from which also we eagerly await a Savior, the Lord Jesus Christ.

1 Thes. 5:9-10 For God did not appoint us to wrath but to the obtaining of salvation through our Lord Jesus Christ, who died for us in order that whether we watch or sleep, we may live together with Him.

_____
Date

Week 4 — Day 1   Today's verses

Rev. 2:26 And he who overcomes and he who keeps My works until the end, to him I will give authority over the nations.

28 And to him I will give the morning star.

22:16 I Jesus have sent My angel to testify to you these things for the churches. I am the Root and the Offspring of David, the bright morning star.

19:7 Let us rejoice and exult, and let us give the glory to Him, for the marriage of the Lamb has come, and His wife has made herself ready.

_____
Date

Week 4 — Day 2   Today's verses

Rev. 19:8-9 And it was given to her that she should be clothed in fine linen, bright and clean; for the fine linen is the righteousnesses of the saints. And he said to me, Write, Blessed are they who are called to the marriage dinner of the Lamb. And he said to me, These are the true words of God.

14:15 And another angel came out of the temple, crying with a loud voice to Him who sat on the cloud, Send forth Your sickle and reap, for the hour to reap has come because the harvest of the earth is ripe.

_____
Date

Week 4 — Day 3   Today's verses

Rev. 3:3 ...If therefore you will not watch, I will come as a thief, and you shall by no means know at what hour I will come upon you.

16:15 Behold, I come as a thief. Blessed is he who watches and keeps his garments that he may not walk naked and they see his shame.

22:12 Behold, I come quickly, and My reward is with Me to render to each one as his work is.

_____
Date

Week 5 — Day 4 — Today's verses

Exo. 25:38 And its tongs and its firepans shall be of pure gold.

39 It shall be made of a talent of pure gold, with all these utensils.

Phil. 2:15 That you may be blameless and guileless, children of God without blemish in the midst of a crooked and perverted generation, among whom you shine as luminaries in the world.

_____
Date

Week 5 — Day 5 — Today's verses

Zech. 4:6 And he answered and spoke to me, saying, This is the word of Jehovah to Zerubbabel, saying, Not by might nor by power, but by My Spirit, says Jehovah of hosts.

Rev. 4:5 ...And *there were* seven lamps of fire burning before the throne, which are the seven Spirits of God.

5:6 And I saw in the midst of the throne and of the four living creatures and in the midst of the elders a Lamb standing as having *just* been slain, having seven horns and seven eyes, which are the seven Spirits of God sent forth into all the earth.

_____
Date

Week 5 — Day 6 — Today's verses

Prov. 20:27 The spirit of man is the lamp of Jehovah, searching all the innermost parts [rooms] of the inner being.

Rev. 4:5 ...And *there were* seven lamps of fire burning before the throne, which are the seven Spirits of God.

1 Cor. 6:17 But he who is joined to the Lord is one spirit.

_____
Date

Week 5 — Day 1 — Today's verses

Exo. 25:31 And you shall make a lampstand of pure gold. The lampstand *with* its base and its shaft shall be made of beaten work; its cups, its calyxes, and its blossom buds shall be of *one piece with* it.

Rev. 1:20 The mystery of...the seven golden lampstands....The seven lampstands are the seven churches.

_____
Date

Week 5 — Day 2 — Today's verses

Exo. 25:31 And you shall make a lampstand of pure gold. The lampstand *with* its base and its shaft shall be made of beaten work; its cups, its calyxes, and its blossom buds shall be of *one piece with* it.

39 It shall be made of a talent of pure gold....

John 4:24 God is Spirit, and those who worship Him must worship in spirit and truthfulness.

_____
Date

Week 5 — Day 3 — Today's verses

Exo. 25:31 And you shall make a lampstand of pure gold. The lampstand *with* its base and its shaft shall be made of beaten work; its cups, its calyxes, and its blossom buds shall be of *one piece with* it.

Phil. 3:10 To know Him and the power of His resurrection and the fellowship of His sufferings, being conformed to His death.

Col. 2:19 ...Holding the Head, out from whom all the Body, being richly supplied and knit together by means of the joints and sinews, grows with the growth of God.

_____
Date

Week 6 — Day 4 — Today's verses

Rev. And His head and hair were like white as
1:14 white wool, as snow; and His eyes were like a flame of fire.

5:6 And I saw in the midst of the throne...a Lamb standing as having *just* been slain, having seven horns and seven eyes, which are the seven Spirits of God sent forth into all the earth.

Dan. His body also was like beryl, His face like
10:6 the appearance of lightning, His eyes like torches of fire....

_____
Date

Week 6 — Day 5 — Today's verses

Rev. And His feet were like shining bronze, as
1:15 having been fired in a furnace; and His voice was like the sound of many waters.

16 And He had in His right hand seven stars....

2:1 ...These things says He who holds the seven stars in His right hand, He who walks in the midst of the seven golden lampstands.

_____
Date

Week 6 — Day 6 — Today's verses

Rev. ...And out of His mouth proceeded a
1:16 sharp two-edged sword; and His face *shone* as the sun shines in its power.

17 And when I saw Him, I fell at His feet as dead; and He placed His right hand on me, saying, Do not fear; I am the First and the Last

18 And the living One; and I became dead, and behold, I am living forever and ever; and I have the keys of death and of Hades.

_____
Date

Week 6 — Day 1 — Today's verses

Rev. And I turned to see the voice that spoke
1:12 with me; and when I turned, I saw seven golden lampstands,

13 And in the midst of the lampstands One like the Son of Man, clothed with a garment reaching to the feet, and girded about at the breasts with a golden girdle.

_____
Date

Week 6 — Day 2 — Today's verses

Rev. And in the midst of the lampstands One
1:13 like the Son of Man, clothed with a garment reaching to the feet, and girded about at the breasts with a golden girdle.

Eph. For no one ever hated his own flesh, but
5:29 nourishes and cherishes it, even as Christ also the church.

30 Because we are members of His Body.

Heb. For we do not have a High Priest who
4:15 cannot be touched with the feeling of our weaknesses, but One who has been tempted in all respects like *us*, yet without sin.

_____
Date

Week 6 — Day 3 — Today's verses

Rev. ...To him who overcomes, to him I will
2:7 give to eat of the tree of life, which is in the Paradise of God.

17 ...To him who overcomes, to him I will give of the hidden manna....

3:20 Behold, I stand at the door and knock; if anyone hears My voice and opens the door, then I will come in to him and dine with him and he with Me.

_____
Date